DEEP LEARNING
FOR A DIGITAL AGE

DEEP LEARNING FOR A DIGITAL AGE

Technology's
Untapped Potential
to Enrich Higher Education

Van B. Weigel

JOSSEY-BASS
A Wiley Company
www.josseybass.com

Published by

 JOSSEY-BASS
A Wiley Company
989 Market Street
San Francisco, CA 94103-1741

www.josseybass.com

Jossey-Bass books and products are available through most bookstores. To contact Jossey-Bass
directly, call (888) 378-2537, fax to (800) 605-2665, or visit our website at www.josseybass.com.

Substantial discounts on bulk quantities of Jossey-Bass books are available to corporations, professional associations, and other organizations. For details and discount information, contact the
special sales department at Jossey-Bass.

We at Jossey-Bass strive to use the most environmentally sensitive paper stocks available to us. Our publi-
cations are printed on acid-free recycled stock whenever possible, and our paper always meets or exceeds
minimum GPO and EPA requirements.

Library of Congress Cataloging-in-Publication Data

Weigel, Van B., 1954–
   Deep learning for a digital age : technology's untapped
potential to enrich higher education / Van B. Weigel.—1st ed.
        p. cm.
Includes bibliographical references and index.
   ISBN 0-7879-5613-9
   1. Education, Higher—Data processing.   2. Education,
Higher—Effect of technological innovations on.   3. Internet in
education.   I. Title.
   LB2395.7 .W45 2002
   378′.00285—dc21
                                                                        2001002783

FIRST EDITION
HB Printing   10 9 8 7 6 5 4 3 2 1

THE JOSSEY-BASS

HIGHER AND ADULT EDUCATION SERIES

CONTENTS

TABLES, FIGURES, AND EXHIBITS

Tables

Figures

Exhibits

PREFACE

Reflective thinking is an art. One learns to think by tapping into one's reservoir of curiosity and setting a course for discovery—mapping unfamiliar landscapes, appraising ideas critically, weighing alternatives, discerning where core values lie. Learning the art of thinking requires the assistance of those who are more skilled by virtue of their knowledge and experience. One does not learn how to play a musical instrument by reading about it or attending a concert; similarly, the art of thinking requires firsthand observation and takes practice.

If temples were built to pay homage to the art of thinking, they would look more like colleges and universities than any other social institution. Libraries and museums contain vast knowledge resources and chronicle abundant achievements in technology and art, but the responsibility to cultivate and nurture thought is the preserve of higher education. Elementary and secondary institutions are also charged with this task, but institutions of higher education must necessarily lead the way.

The central argument of this book is that the use of technology in higher education should enrich and extend the student's exploration of new territory. Educational technologies are of little value if they do not add richness and dimensionality to the experience of learning. Education is not about earning a credential, stuffing information into one's head, or performing well on an exam. It is about seeing familiar landscapes in a new light, discovering something new in the world or in oneself, and experiencing the satisfaction of becoming good at something.

This book outlines a decentralized learning architecture for higher education that blends classroom-based education with e-learning—a bricks-and-clicks approach. I use the term *depth education* to refer to this model. The approach emphasizes the use of collaborative virtual spaces—called knowledge rooms—as a kind of matrix for deep learning. Knowledge rooms are to the teacher what the canvas is to the artist; there is no need to interpose layers of curriculum developers, computer professionals, and graphic artists between instructors and their students.

I define deep learning as *learning that promotes the development of conditionalized knowledge and metacognition through communities of inquiry.* Deep learning, of course, does not require e-learning in any fashion. Ph.D. programs and medical schools are exceptionally successful examples of deep learning, and they have been around for a lot longer than the Internet. The significance of e-learning is that it makes possible something that would not otherwise be feasible from a logistical or economic standpoint. We may well be in the initial stages of a revolution in learning that combines richness with accessibility and in so doing parts company with the dominant educational motif of surface learning.

The idea that both quality and accessibility can be improved simultaneously has come to be a hallmark of Internet technologies. This phenomenon has been well documented by Philip Evans and Thomas Wurster (2000) of the Boston Consulting Group. They argue that the significance of the Internet—an invention on the scale of Gutenberg's—is that it "blows up" the existing trade-off between richness and reach, making it possible to attain higher levels of richness and reach with the same bundle of economic resources. Richness refers to the overall quality of information (for example, its currency, accuracy, interactivity, relevance), and reach refers to the number of people involved in the exchange of information.

What is striking about the usual response of institutions of higher education in this new economic environment is their near universal fixation on the reach side of the trade-off. The effect is to make e-learning hostage to distance education. Instead of focusing on how the experience of learning can be enriched through Internet technologies, many institutions are preoccupied with how distance education makes it possible for them to defer the construction of new dorms and parking lots or to reach educational markets on the other side of the planet. This is a grave strategic error (Weigel, 2000a, 2000b). I hope that this book will help educators, and those charged with the oversight of institutions of higher education, to grapple with the issues that higher education will confront in the twenty-first century.

Chapter One, "Beyond the Virtual Classroom," introduces the concept of deep learning and explores it in the larger contexts of social constructivism and the learning methodology known as cognitive apprenticeship. The chapter then presents two key aspects of depth education—the cultivation of intellectual curiosity and the curricular implementation of embedded assessment—and introduces the knowledge room concept. Knowledge rooms are collaborative, virtual spaces where students gather for research projects, skill development, seminar discussions, formal debates, and creative expression. Five types of knowledge rooms are introduced here: the Research Center, the Skill Workplace, the Conference Center, the Debate Hall, and the Portfolio Gallery. The chapter concludes with a review of hybrid or blended approaches to e-learning and a brief reflection on the alleged resistance of educators to new instructional technologies.

Chapter Two, "The Commoditization of Instruction," offers a critique of distance education and computer-based learning in light of the long-term trend of the commoditization of instruction. Commoditization is the process in which products or services become standardized to the extent that their attributes are roughly the same. Two factors, in particular, have facilitated this process in instruction: a minimalist definition of learning that focuses on information transfer, and the widespread use of adjunct faculty to reduce the costs of instruction. Unfortunately, institutions of higher education have proceeded uncritically down the path of commoditizing instruction, and this greatly increases their vulnerability. The chapter proceeds with an analysis of how the broadband virtual classroom, made possible by the growth of residential broadband Internet access, poses a threat to colleges and universities that rely on a surface approach to learning. The broadband virtual classroom will not only render the standard narrowband approaches to distance education obsolete but also surpass the interactivity of the large lecture classroom while capitalizing on the economies of scale made possible by the Internet. If we factor in the likely growth of e-commerce, this may portend an era of tuition-free college degrees. The chapter concludes with an assessment of the opportunities and challenges associated with the broadband virtual classroom. The recent experience of *Encyclopedia Britannica* is instructive in this regard.

Chapter Three, "Transforming the Classroom into Knowledge Rooms," details the knowledge room concept of depth education and elaborates its pedagogical significance in light of the methodology of cognitive apprenticeship. Institutions of higher education have adopted an assembly line approach to education that perhaps fits well with an industrial economy but is out of step with the knowledge-based New Economy. Knowledge management is a core skill of the New Economy, and it requires discernment and discovery rather than absorption and recall. A work group paradigm for the classroom is presented, and it is argued that this approach, which relies strongly on virtual teams, has the advantage of removing the instructor from the center of classroom interactions. From there, the chapter explores how the flexible and decentralized structure of depth education can facilitate grassroots change in educational institutions. The remainder of the chapter focuses on a detailed description of each knowledge room and its pedagogical features.

Chapter Four, "Building an Infrastructure for Depth Education," explores the infrastructure requirements for depth education. The infrastructure requirements of depth education are primarily conceptual, and they begin with faculty. In particular, faculty development initiatives in five areas are of special importance: confronting the crowding-out effect, offering formative evaluation, working with virtual teams, developing weaving skills, and understanding copyright law. From there, the chapter explores the importance of the campus library and its staff for depth education. This discussion focuses on the overall pattern of disinvestment in library acquisitions and notes several of the difficulties of the grand vision of a digital library. A hybrid, just-in-time approach is recommended as the most realistic alternative. From there, the chapter examines the technical infrastructure needed for depth education, focusing on computer hardware, network capacity, and technical support. The chapter concludes with a discussion of five technological developments that will significantly enhance the scope and quality of depth education: residential broadband Internet access, voice over IP (VOIP), near flawless voice recognition, videoconferencing, and electronic books.

Finally, Chapter Five, "New Horizons for Higher Education," describes some of the educational vistas made possible by e-learning and the knowledge room framework of depth education. Beginning with a reflection on the digital divide and the mission of higher education in bridging it, the chapter explores the promising concept of the international distributed campus. Not a few academic institutions will find the international distributed campus to be an exciting and economically viable option in the global educational marketplace. The chapter proceeds to explore several key downstream and upstream services that colleges and universities can offer to enhance the value of their degree programs and educational offerings. The chapter concludes with a reflection on the importance of wisdom as a curricular aspiration for higher education. Although wisdom can in no way be programmed into a curriculum, it is possible to create learning environments that nurture its development by reflecting on the larger meaning and significance of a student's encounters with new knowledge.

Acknowledgments

In writing this book, I owe a great debt of gratitude to my teachers over the years. I would be especially remiss not to mention Thomas McDaniel and Culbert Rutenber. They have modeled a transformational approach to education that escapes definition but grows in influence with each passing year. I am also grateful to Elizabeth Morgan, one of my colleagues at Eastern, who took a junior faculty member patiently under her wing and has never failed to respond compassionately when I fell short. Most of what I have learned about teaching has come as a direct result of our collaboration in the classroom. I would also like to thank Vivian Nix-Early for her unwavering support for my sabbatical project, which became this book, and my wife, Linda, who cheerfully endured the competing demands on my time and has always sought the best for me. Special thanks are also due to Norma Thomasson for her careful proofing of the manuscript. Finally, I owe a word of appreciation to Theodore Marchese for his timely words of encouragement and to Gale Erlandson for her thoughtful editorial guidance and enthusiastic support of this project.

Van B. Weigel
St. Davids, Pennsylvania
August 2001

For my nieces, Julie and Melissa . . .
may learning never lose its intrigue.

THE AUTHOR

Van B. Weigel is professor of ethics and economic development at Eastern College in St. Davids, Pennsylvania (vweigel@eastern.edu). He earned a Ph.D. in ethics and society from the University of Chicago (1987) and is the author of *A Unified Theory of Global Development* (1989), a *Choice* Outstanding Academic Book, and *Earth Cancer* (1995). He has published articles in *World Development*, the *Chronicle of Higher Education*, and *Change*.

He resides in West Chester, Pennsylvania, with his wife, Linda Thomasson.

DEEP LEARNING
FOR A DIGITAL AGE

CHAPTER ONE

BEYOND THE VIRTUAL CLASSROOM

"For on-line education to become mainstream is kind of a depressing thought, because it is such a crappy experience. The bottom line is that learning on-line is a soul-destroying experience. It really, really stinks. It's always second best" (Hamilton, 2001, p. R32). These words, published recently in the *Wall Street Journal*, were not spoken by an irate faculty member or a closet Luddite. The speaker, Marc Eisenstadt, is the chief scientist of the Knowledge Media Institute of the United Kingdom's Open University. The Open University has used on-line education to supplement its extension courses and correspondence programs since the mid-1990s, and Eisenstadt's institute conducts research on distance education and virtual classrooms. His blunt assessment is part of the larger reassessment of the Internet that has been taking place since the fall of the NASDAQ in April 2000 and the dot-com meltdown that followed. The business community, confronting the sobering reality of stock valuations that have fallen to sub-basement levels, is returning to the old-fashioned virtue of economic performance over market potential. E-learning must be scrutinized with the same healthy skepticism. Will e-learning really deliver, or will it turn out to be just another casualty of the overblown expectations of the late 1990s?

This book is about a simple idea. Technology should enrich the experience of learning. E-learning technologies may save some costs and add a measure of convenience, but if they do not deepen the learning experiences of students, they are not worth much.

John Chambers, CEO of Cisco Systems, the company most responsible for supplying the electronic plumbing that runs the Internet, hails e-learning as "the next big wave in Internet-based applications" (D'Amico, 1999). More recently, Sean Maloney, executive vice president of Intel, proclaimed that e-learning "will be the killer application over the next two to three years" (Mannion, 2001). They may be right. But e-learning will fall far short of its potential if it merely repackages our current educational models in digital format. Instead, it should enable students to become more proficient learners.

Nearly all varieties of distance education have failed to bring depth and dimensionality to the experience of learning. With the exception of a few innovative firms like Cognitive Arts and UNext.com, most distance education providers are serving up variants of a "post-a-lecture" and "host-a-discussion" approach. The differences between them are not worth mentioning. The basic idea is to port the classroom to the Internet in the most efficient way possible—not unlike software engineers porting software programs to different operating environments. One company even promises to put entire campuses on-line in sixty business days! Could something that is really valuable be accomplished that quickly? One suspects that many distance education initiatives are the result of little more than an impulsive game of keeping up with the Joneses—motivated more by the primordial fear of being left behind than by a desire to apply sound pedagogical method.

Even popular classroom-based instructional technologies (the ubiquitous PowerPoint presentation, for example) have treated the computer as little more than an overhead projector with bells and whistles. It may be argued that compelling graphics and arresting slide transitions help keep the attention of students in a lecture hall (unless they are sitting in a darkened classroom right after lunch). But if a technology can secure a student's heightened interest in a lecture, does it also enhance his or her ability to learn? That student may have more accurate and well-organized lecture notes or be better able to recall material during an exam, but is this what learning is all about?

Deep Learning and the Construction of Knowledge

Deep learning finds its inspiration in a school of educational thought known as constructivism, and in particular, the branch of constructivist thought known as *social constructivism*.[1]

Stemming from the work of Jean Piaget and Lev Vygotsky, and drawing inspiration from John Dewey's focus on active learning, constructivism holds that all knowledge is constructed based on the experiences and cognitive structures that are available to us. Reality becomes sensible and coherent because we construct it. Knowledge is not something that bombards our consciousness and is absorbed; rather, it is something that we actively construct to make the world meaningful. Learning involves a search for new knowledge—or "new territory"—that is strongly related to the activities of play, discovery, and problem solving. According to the constructivist standpoint, instructors cannot walk into the classroom and presume anything like a preexisting thirst for knowledge. Instead, they must create a discovery-based learning environment that launches students on a search for new territory.

The best place to see constructivist thinking at work is not in the classroom but in those high-tech firms that encourage playfulness to induce creativity. In a survey of the work environments of high-tech firms that he carried out for the *Washington Post,* Dale Russakoff (2000) observed that from "workers sprawled on their stomachs using laptops, to employee playrooms full of Legos and easels, to the rebellion against hierarchy, the culture of the new economy makes work feel unmistakably like play. Consciously or unconsciously, it recalls the atmosphere of early childhood—the stage of human life when the learning curve is the steepest and the pace of learning is unrivaled."

Knowledge constructions, or what Piaget called *schema,* are the central building blocks of constructivism. They refer to ways of perceiving and thinking that make the world meaningful to us. Our knowledge of the world is based entirely on these knowledge constructions; we have no other avenue for accessing information about the world. Because each person's experiences are unique, the knowledge constructions that each person creates to bring understanding and coherence to the world may differ significantly from the knowledge constructions of others. For example, people who speak the same language and have received formal training in mathematics may have similar knowledge constructions when it comes to the ordering of words or manipulation of numbers. But such similarities fade quickly when the discussion turns to spiritual experience or moral obligation.

Constructivism, therefore, presumes that people will process new information differently and places great value on dialogical processes. Differences in perspectives are approached with a presumption of humility. In this respect, there are many similarities between constructivism as an educational philosophy and postmodernist thought.[2]

Learning, according to Piaget (1970), takes place through the interplay of two polar forces: assimilation and accommodation. These forces are kept in balance by an adaptive and dynamic process of equilibration (Piaget, 1977). *Assimilation* refers to the process by which the learners incorporate new information and experiences into the framework of their preexisting knowledge constructions, thereby rendering the unfamiliar familiar. When learners have new experiences or are exposed to ideas that cannot be squared with their knowledge constructions, they must explore new territory in an effort to resolve the dissonance or contradiction in their minds. Doing this requires some thought. *Accommodation* takes place when learners accommodate these new experiences or ideas by bringing their knowledge constructions in line with the new information.

Lev Vygotsky (1978, 1986), a Russian developmental psychologist, brought a distinct social dimension to constructivism. Vygotsky focused on the way that language, culture, and social interactions affect learning processes. He distinguished between what he called spontaneous and scientific concepts. *Spontaneous concepts* are similar to Piaget's notion of knowledge structures. These ideas and understandings bubble up spontaneously from the learner's own reflections on everyday life. *Scientific concepts,* by contrast, are more formal and abstract in character and can be conveyed through classroom instruction. Scientific concepts work their way down into the learner's consciousness by supplying the learner with conceptual resources that assist him or her in constructing spontaneous knowledge structures that are more comprehensive and adequate.

The meeting place between spontaneous and scientific concepts is what Vygotsky referred to as the *zone of proximal development*. Because each learner brings different sets of spontaneous concepts into the classroom, this zone will vary from one individual to the next. It is in this zone that the learner's ability to solve problems independently is enhanced through "collaboration with more able peers" (Vygotsky, 1978, p. 86). Hence, Vygotsky recognized the important contributions of both teacher and learning community in intellectual development.

It is hardly a coincidence that the ancient model of apprenticeship not only relies on the observation of expert performance by the novice but also rests upon considerable interactions among peers. As Barbara Rogoff (1990, p. 39) notes, "The apprenticeship model has the value of including more people than a single expert and a single novice; the apprenticeship system often involves a group of novices (peers) who serve as resources for one another in exploring the new domain and aiding and challenging one another. . . . Hence the model provided by apprenticeship is one of active learners in a community of people who support, challenge, and guide novices as they increasingly participate in skilled, valued sociocultural activity."

The familiar debate over process versus content loses relevance in a constructivist perspective (Marlowe and Page, 1998). Content is the medium for knowledge construction and the springboard for learning. But merely possessing information does little to advance the goals of education. Learning, from the standpoint of constructivism, takes place when students act on content, when they shape and form it. Content is the clay of knowledge construction; learning takes place when it is fashioned into something meaningful. Creativity, critical analysis, and skillful performance are inextricably linked to the process of creating more viable and coherent knowledge structures.

Defining Deep Learning

The broad concepts of constructivism have gained ample support through research over the past thirty years in developmental psychology, cognitive psychology, and more recently, neuroscience. It is now possible to speak credibly of an emergent science of learning. The Committee on Developments in the Science of Learning of the National Research Council has assembled and analyzed the primary conclusions of this research in an elegant volume entitled *How People Learn*, published by National Academy Press (Bransford, Brown, and Cocking, 1999).

The recent developments in neuroscience are particularly striking. Technologies such as positron emission tomography (PET) and functional magnetic resonance imaging (fMRI) have extended our understanding of some of the brain's learning mechanisms. Because of this work, we now know that learning actually modifies the physical structure of the brain. Among the most basic rules of learning is that "practice increases learning and that there is a corresponding relationship between the amount of experience in a complex environment and the amount of structural change in the brain" (Bransford, Brown, and Cocking, 1999, p. xvi; see also pp. 102–115).

Drawing on the core themes of *How People Learn*, I define deep learning as *learning that promotes the development of conditionalized knowledge and metacognition through communities of inquiry.* Throughout this book I use the term *depth education* to refer to the particular model of deep learning developed in this book.[3] Table 1.1 presents a brief comparison of deep versus surface learning.

Although there is no intrinsic connection between deep learning and e-learning, the two are intertwined in the depth education model presented here. From a practical standpoint, deep learning and e-learning are inseparable. It is simply not economically feasible to provide a broad cross section of students with depth educational curricula unless Internet technologies are used. If medical schools and top-tier Ph.D. programs are seen as examples of how deep learning can be successfully embedded into a traditional academic curricula, then our experience to date is that deep learning does not come cheap. Hence, technology becomes a critical factor.

Deep learning is rooted in the formation of conditionalized knowledge, metacognition, and communities of inquiry.

Table 1.1. DEEP LEARNING VERSUS SURFACE LEARNING

Attributes of Deep Learning	Attributes of Surface Learning
Learners relate ideas to previous knowledge and experience.	Learners treat the course as unrelated bits of knowledge.
Learners look for patterns and underlying principles.	Learners memorize facts and carry out procedures routinely.
Learners check evidence and relate it to conclusions.	Learners find difficulty in making sense of new ideas presented.
Learners examine logic and argument cautiously and critically.	Learners see little value or meaning in either courses or tasks.
Learners are aware of the understanding that develops while learning.	Learners study without reflecting on either purpose or strategy.
Learners become actively interested in the course content.	Learners feel undue pressure and worry about work.

Source: Adapted from Entwistle, 2001.

Conditionalized Knowledge

Conditionalized knowledge refers to knowledge that specifies the contexts in which it is useful. It is knowledge that recognizes its own limitations. Students gain conditionalized knowledge only when they have the opportunity to apply disciplinary concepts and methodologies to varied contexts and knowledge domains.

Surface learning, by contrast, focuses on mere description and textbook application of disciplinary concepts and methodologies. It offers little opportunity for students to discern when those concepts and methodologies are relevant to more realistic problems and other knowledge domains. The authors of *How People Learn* note, "Many forms of curricula and instruction do not help students conditionalize their knowledge. . . . It is left largely to students to generate the condition-action pairs required for solving novel problems" (Bransford, Brown, and Cocking, 1999, p. 31).

Problem-based learning is a key instructional strategy for the development of conditionalized knowledge. It not only has the advantage of introducing ideas "when students see a need or reason for their use" (Bransford, Brown, and Cocking, 1999, p. 127) but also emphasizes the relevance of course content to real life, thus imbuing instructional objectives with instant credibility. For example, the physician's ability to diagnose medical problems is enhanced when medical students are exposed to problem-based learning, in place of traditional lectures, during the first year of medical school (Hmelo, 1995). It is no coincidence that forward-looking distance learning initiatives—like Cognitive Arts (working with Columbia and Harvard) and UNext.com (involving Carnegie Mellon University,

Columbia University, the London School of Economics and Political Science, Stanford University, and the University of Chicago)—use a problem-solving format for their courses instead of traditional lectures and readings (Carr, 2000d; Gajilan, 2001; McCormick, 2000).

If faculty understand their teaching responsibilities primarily in terms of "covering the material," that leaves them with little time and energy to help students to conditionalize their knowledge of a discipline. This sacrifice of depth for breadth is a prominent characteristic of most higher education curricula. Textbook publishers who seek to differentiate their offerings in the marketplace by adding new and more advanced topics to each successive edition exacerbate this problem. Even sensible instructors who respond to this kind of content inflation by making selective use of textbook material do not have the advantage of building out from a depth treatment of a discipline.

Metacognition

Metacognition refers to the ability to think about thinking—the art of thinking. It involves being able to monitor and reflect on one's level of understanding, to know when this understanding is not adequate, and to know how to remedy this inadequacy (Bransford, Brown, and Cocking, 1999). Metacognition is about developing students' own self-awareness as learners and empowering them to manage their own development as learners—learning how to learn. The development of critical thinking skills and the ability to articulate and reflect on ideas are foundational to the art of thinking. Furthermore, students who develop their metacognitive skills are better able to transfer learning that takes place in one knowledge domain to other domains.

Communities of Inquiry

I use the term *communities of inquiry* to refer to communities of practice (or learning communities) in academic settings (see Wenger, 1998). Much learning in everyday life takes place in communities of practice (Lave and Wenger, 1993; Wenger, 1998; Wenger and Snyder, 2000). These formal and informal communities crisscross the entirety of social life and are particularly important for the experience of learning (Brown and Duguid, 1996).

One could argue that the genius of the residential college experience is that it places students in a rich array of intersecting communities of practice organized around the themes of intellectual, social, and personal development. As Gregory Farrington (1999), the president of Lehigh University, notes:

Undergraduate life at a residential college is as much about learning to live as it is about learning from books. What is most impressive about the residential college experience is that it works so well and achieves both goals so effectively. Eighteen-year-old students nervously tiptoe onto campus at the start of their first year, and four years later they march out—sometimes after a bit of prodding, to be sure, but generally with the motivation, education, and confidence needed to take on the world. The transformation is remarkable and is as much the product of the general intellectual and social experience on-campus as the result of what goes on formally in the classroom. For these students, late-night discussions are much of what college is about, and the role of the football team is truly important.

Although older students in traditional graduate programs or nontraditional adult education programs hardly require the diverse array of communities of practice that are found in an undergraduate environment, it would be a serious mistake to discount the value of more focused *communities of inquiry* for their educational experience. From graduate students debating an arcane disciplinary issue over a pitcher of beer to a close-knit cohort of working professionals in an accelerated MBA program, communities of inquiry play an important role in adding depth to and contextualizing an academic curriculum.

As Brown and Duguid (2000) emphasize, learning involves a process of "enculturation" that engages students with concepts and communities of practice. "Teaching and education, from this perspective, are not simply matters of putting students in touch with information. . . . Rather, they are matters of putting students in touch with particular communities. The university's great advantage is that it can put learners in touch with communities that they don't know about" (p. 220).

It is interesting that Carole Fungaroli, author of *Traditional Degrees for Nontraditional Students* (2000), urges working adults to attend college but warns students against distance education. The on-line students whom she has encountered report an educational experience marked by discouragement and isolation: "They hated what they were doing, but they just wanted to get those three credit hours" ("New Book Says," 1999, p. A47). The virtual campus, according to Fungaroli, fails to deliver the most important aspect of higher education—inspiration.

"At its best, the traditional campus can make you fall in love with something. One of the things missing from the distance learning area is passion. . . . When you get on campus, you might find out that you're all fired up about something that you might not have thought about before. Distance learning allows you to stay in your rut" (p. A47).

Deep Learning and Cognitive Apprenticeship

Cognitive apprenticeship is the learning methodology best suited to achieve the aims of deep learning. This approach attempts to integrate the salient features of the apprenticeship model—which has proven so effective in transmitting skills down through the generations—into the structure of a formal curriculum. From the perspective of cognitive apprenticeship, the art of thinking is no different than the art of becoming a musician or a surgeon.

In their seminal article on cognitive apprenticeship, John Seely Brown, Allan Collins, and Paul Duguid (1989) observe that the development of knowledge proficiencies is very similar to the manner in which artisans learn to use a tool. One does not become an artisan by merely possessing a tool and being acquainted with its function, and the same is true for those who acquire knowledge (that is, facts, definitions, concepts, and methodologies) but really cannot use it.

> People who use tools actively rather than just acquire them . . . build an increasingly rich implicit understanding of the world in which they use the tools and of the tools themselves. The understanding, both of the world and of the tool, continually changes as a result of their interaction. . . .
>
> Learning how to use a tool involves far more than can be accounted for in any set of rules. The occasions and conditions for use arise directly out of the context of activities of each community that uses the tool, framed by the way members of that community see the world. . . . Because tools and the way they are used reflect the particular accumulated insights of communities, it is not possible to use a tool appropriately without understanding the community or culture in which it is used. [p. 33]

The concept of cognitive apprenticeship modifies the traditional apprenticeship model in three important respects. First, cognitive apprenticeship is focused on the development of cognitive skills, or the art of thinking, and not on skills associated with a specific craft or attached to particular roles in the workplace. Second, cognitive apprenticeship encourages the application of knowledge and skills in a variety of contexts, enabling students to abstract general principles from their experiences of learning by doing. Third, unlike the traditional apprenticeship model, the elements of cognitive apprenticeship can be integrated into a formal curriculum and are not confined to workplace exigencies or the latest fashion in business trends (Collins, Brown, and Newman, 1989). Graduate programs in the sciences are perhaps the closest approximation of the cognitive apprenticeship model in higher education (Brooks, 1996).

Collins, Brown, and Newman (1989) have identified six teaching methods that facilitate cognitive apprenticeship: modeling, coaching, scaffolding, articulating, reflecting, and exploring (see also Collins, 1991; Jonassen, 1996; and Teles, 1993).

Modeling

Modeling is the externalization of internal cognitive processes. Essentially, the teacher puts her mind on display, walking her students through her approach to a problem and making explicit the internal steps she took and strategies she used along the way. Modeling is about teaching students how to think, by means of observation, in order to disclose patterns of thinking and approaches to problem solving. Modeling need not be confined to the teacher's own problem-solving approaches; it should also highlight successful problem-solving approaches developed by students. One might think of modeling as storytelling about problem solving, critical analysis, or the creative development of alternatives.

Coaching

When coaching, the teacher becomes the classroom observer. Whereas modeling emphasizes the student's role as observer, coaching requires teachers to observe students in the performance of some task or skill (usually in the context of problem solving) and to ask questions or to offer feedback on the student's performance. Coaching resembles Socrates' dialogical method in that the teacher adapts her approach based on something that is said or done by the student.

Scaffolding

Scaffolding is a concept drawn from constructivism.[4] It refers to the supporting roles of the teacher and the student's learning community in facilitating the construction of knowledge. This can take the form of a teacher helping a student complete a task that he is unable to perform or building a structure for hints and helps in the curriculum. Scaffolding can also take the form of participating in a community of inquiry that supports the student in the knowledge construction process (Hogan and Pressley, 1997). In this respect, scaffolding can be thought of as building opportunities for student-to-student modeling and coaching in the curriculum.

Articulating

The process of articulation allows students to practice their skills in converting tacit knowledge to explicit knowledge. The effect is to draw out the internal reasoning processes of students by encouraging them to articulate their response to an idea or their approach to a problem. Articulation has other benefits besides the intrinsic rewards of learning how to make tacit knowledge explicit; for example, it makes knowledge more readily available so that it can be employed in different tasks, it helps students apply similar problem solving strategies in different contexts, and it encourages students to see an idea from the perspective of another student (Collins, 1991). Articulation also allows the teacher to draw on the thinking of students to serve as a model for their classmates. In this way, the students' own knowledge contributions become a subject for classroom analysis.

Reflecting

The process of reflection is essentially a debriefing process that can take the form of comparing notes or conducting an "abstracted replay" of one's thought processes. Because reflection encourages students to note the ways in which their performance differs from other students, it helps them compare their own approaches to critical analysis and problem solving with those of other students, as well as the teacher. It is a highly beneficial teaching tool because it makes what the student says or does the object of instruction.

Exploring

Exploring, the final method of cognitive apprenticeship, encourages students to tackle new knowledge domains and problems on their own. One can think of exploration in terms of the progressive withdrawal of the scaffolding intended to support the students. The teacher's role is to encourage students to set achievable goals, to form and test hypotheses, and to make discoveries on their own (Collins, 1991). This responsibility of educators to set students on the search for new territory—in Piaget's words—requires us to reexamine the important role of curiosity in learning.

Deep Learning and Intellectual Curiosity

Curiosity is a fundamental learning skill. Yet it is perhaps the most underrepresented skill in higher education curricula.

It may seem odd to consider curiosity a skill, and yet it is certainly no less a skill than listening, speaking, or writing. Intellectual curiosity—like skills in articulation, reflection, and critical thinking—is learned through observation and practice. One learns (or more accurately, relearns) curiosity by being in the company of the curious. No lecture, textbook, computer program, or Web site can impart this skill. It is learned only through apprenticeship experiences with skillful thinkers and through participation in a community of inquiry.

The lecture, an exceptionally efficient mechanism for conveying information, has many liabilities when it comes to developing the skill of intellectual curiosity. Content is usually presented in pre-packaged doses in a take it or leave it fashion. Consequently, learning in class often becomes little more than an information transaction, where the teacher deposits information into the accounts of students (Freire, 1995).

The use of multimedia technologies in the classroom, like PowerPoint presentations, has only intensified the perception that knowledge is neatly portioned and served up in small bulleted points. The instructor's desire to get through the slides can easily crowd out opportunities to engage students in critical dialogue about the material. Students usually ask questions of clarification instead of probing the overall relevance or adequacy of the discussion at hand. More often than not, the question What will be on the exam? overshadows the larger questions: Why is this material important to me? What are the built-in limitations of this material? How will this material enhance my current skills and knowledge base?

It could be argued that Internet services that pay students to take extensive notes on a professor's lecture in order to make them available to other students on their Web site are responding to a situation created by educators themselves. The furor over posting lecture notes on Web sites is probably related more to the frustration that students can pass a course without attending class than to concerns over theft of intellectual property.[5] Unlike the medieval scholars who lectured in darkened rooms so that their students could not take notes, in order to protect their intellectual property (Shapiro and Varian, 1999), contemporary professors are rarely concerned with students stealing their ideas. Most feel deeply flattered by assiduous note-takers—at least until now.

If class attendance is merely about an information transaction between teacher and student, then posting lecture notes on the Internet makes perfect sense. Students' skipping class and getting notes from the Internet is more intellectually honest than the teacher force-feeding information to students and looking the other way while students multitask the classroom environment.

Multitasking means doing several things at once. One has to spend only a few minutes in a typical lecture class—particularly a large one—to observe that attentive listeners and note-takers are in short supply. Daydreaming, reading assignments for other classes, writing notes to friends, and catching up on needed sleep are more common classroom activities. High-tech classrooms may be more appealing, but they also provide more sophisticated multitasking opportunities. For example, it is not unheard of for students at Columbia University's School of Business to interrupt a lecture with whoops of joy or anguished sighs. Yet the content of the professor's lecture has nothing to do with these outbursts. Instead, students are responding to the stock trades they are conducting on their computers (Wilgoren, 2000). A professor at Yale Law School recently lamented in the editorial pages of the *New York Times* that his students "went ballistic" when he requested that laptop computers be used for note-taking and not for playing video games or surfing the Web (Ayres, 2001).

Often the only real opportunity to set one's curiosity free in the traditional college classroom is while writing a research paper. Although most professors welcome papers that are creative, innovative, and show some risk-taking, the die is cast by the time the student gets around to choosing a topic and writing the paper. All the incentives are in place to reward those who pick manageable topics—which translates roughly to "It's been done hundreds of times before" and "It's best to play it safe."

It is not surprising that such research exercises have become so superficial that it is easy to get prepackaged research papers over the Internet from term paper mills. These sites allegedly offer materials for background research, but Internet URLs like www.schoolsucks.com and www.cheater.com leave nothing to the imagination. There are even Web-based services, like Plagiarism.org or IntegriGuard (www.integriguard.com), that analyze student papers against a broad database of sample research papers for the purpose of alerting professors to plagiarized material (Carnevale, 1999c; Guernsey, 1998b).

What is remarkable about all this is not that some students seek the easy way out but rather the pronounced lack of imagination in the design of research assignments, which permits the recycling of the same material year after year with little difficulty. Educators' attempts to cope with the problem by using electronic plagiarism services will ultimately have a corrosive effect by extending the hermeneutic of suspicion to the teacher-student relationship.

Deep Learning and Embedded Assessment

A robust assessment strategy is required in order to build vital communities of inquiry. Apart from the process of honest and constructive feedback, talk of learning community is vacuous, amounting to little more than a support group of the ten-steps variety. An assessment strategy that focuses on summative evaluation, rather than formative assessment, denies students meaningful opportunities for intellectual challenge and growth.

Depth education uses an assessment model that I call *embedded evaluation*.[6] Embedded evaluation proceeds from three foundational principles: (1) learning to assess others can be just as helpful as receiving assessment; (2) assessment should have both a private and a public dimension; and (3) evaluations should not be anonymous.

First Principle

The first principle of embedded evaluation emphasizes the value of giving and getting criticism in a respectful and gracious manner. This is no small task! There is an abundance of anecdotal evidence that electronic exchanges of a critical nature between students often appear harsh and inconsiderate. The emotional restraints built into face-to-face communication are largely absent from such exchanges, and in addition, the resources of gesture, voice, and inflection are not there to soften the rough edges of critical words. Because no one cares to be insulted, individuals who are adept at using words to convey both the intended meaning and a respectful tone will have a better than even chance of succeeding in the collaborative atmosphere of the twenty-first-century workplace. Gartner predicts that by 2004, virtual teams will be doing 80 percent of the knowledge-related work in the world's 2000 largest companies (Prencipe, 2001). Even if videoconferencing becomes widespread, it will only supplement—not supplant—text-based electronic communication. The ability to use text-based communication to assert opinion, offer recommendations, and convey nuance will only grow in importance in the coming years.

Second Principle

The second principle of embedded assessment is that assessment should have both a private and a public dimension. The evaluation of individual work must necessarily be "for your eyes only"—accessible only to the instructor and the student who is being evaluated. By contrast, the evaluation of collaborative work products should be a kind of community property of the entire class. Such a peer-to-team assessment model also facilitates the use of guest evaluators (for example, selected alumni, faculty from other departments) to add depth and diversity to the evaluation process.

Third Principle

The third principle of embedded assessment is that neither individual nor group evaluations should be anonymous. The primary failing of anonymous evaluations is that they do not facilitate responsible feedback and prepare students for performance evaluations in the real world. In addition, they limit the instructor's ability to factor the quality of a student's evaluation of others into his or her own course grade. In order to reduce the natural discomfort associated with submitting an evaluation with one's name on it, the instructor should emphasize the importance of constructive feedback in the learning process and the need to balance negative assessments with positive comments and suggestions.

The Shortcomings of Standard Assessment

Because embedded evaluation seeks to measure a student's progress in developing conditionalized knowledge and metacognitive skills, it places considerable weight on the student's ability to articulate and reflect on his own developing knowledge base. This is quite different from standard assessment tools, such as the multiple choice exam, that are inherently indifferent to how and why students arrive at a particular answer. Although well-designed multiple choice exams occasionally succeed in evaluating the reasoning behind an answer, the strategic focus of most students in taking such exams is to stimulate recall and eliminate options. This approach rewards those who are able to absorb and recall information quickly. Such tests send the message to students that the important thing is to recognize the correct answer. This is the "payoff" of a student's toolbox of skills and concepts. Hence, the process of evaluation seems more like a contrived game than an invitation for growth. From this perspective, the well-known tendency of students to forget information quickly after a test is perfectly rational. Why clutter your mind with details whose usefulness largely disappears once you take the exam?

One could argue that distance education programs are well positioned to lead the way in developing effective mechanisms for assessment—particularly project-based assessment tools (Carnevale, 2001a). Yet a pronounced bias in favor of standard assessment tools is evident among distance education providers who boast about the array of nifty tools to create and grade exams of the true-false, multiple choice, matching, and fill-in-the blank varieties. These tools are really only viable for developing practice tests. Graded tests must necessarily be administered in a proctored environment; otherwise, there is nothing to prevent students from keeping their textbook or lecture notes right in front of them when they take the exam.[7] While there is no doubt that practice tests are helpful in preparing for a graded exam, is this really what we mean by formative assessment? Should formative assessment be focused on enhancing a student's exam-taking skills? Or should the focus be placed on how well a student understands a particular knowledge domain and manages the process of learning?

Transforming the Classroom into Knowledge Rooms

The centerpiece of the depth education model presented here is the *knowledge room*—a virtual and collaborative space where students gather for research projects, skill development, seminar discussions, formal debates, and creative expression. This collaborative and project-based approach enables students to hone their skills in research, reflection, analysis, communication, and leadership—skills that are important for many different careers and are necessary in the twenty-first-century workplace. Above all, the knowledge room is a place where the practice of inquiry takes shape. It is designed to supplement, not supplant, the classroom.

Depth education uses five types of knowledge rooms in addition to face-to-face classrooms. Readers are invited to visit www.knowledgeroom.com and to try their hand at constructing their own knowledge rooms. The five knowledge rooms are these: the Research Center, the Skill Workplace, the Conference Center, the Debate Hall, and the Portfolio Gallery.

These primary knowledge rooms may be supplemented with two other rooms: the Map Room, which contains the course syllabus and consolidates in one place all of the "navigational" information needed for the course, including student and faculty bios and an advising area for rapid-response feedback from students concerning the course, and the Assessment Suite, which houses a set of secure spaces, assigned individually to each student, for performance reviews and grade reports.

Knowledge rooms can be thought of as versatile and miniature think tanks that may be active for just a few days or have an effective life span of several years. They may be configured for any number of students. Most knowledge rooms, though, will have fewer than twenty-five students. These virtual spaces may be used as stand-alone components in a course or be assembled in a mix-and-match fashion to fit the instructional aims of the course (see Chizmar and Williams, 2001). Furthermore, a single course can incorporate multiple constructions of each knowledge room type (for example, six Research Centers, eight Skill Workplaces, one Conference Center, six Debate Halls).

The knowledge room framework developed here uses a "self-service" collaboration tool from IBM and the Lotus Development Corporation called Quick-Place. QuickPlace is one of the leading representatives of a software genre called teamware. Teamware is browser-based software that allows end users to build and maintain a secure virtual space for collaborative work, without the intervention of technical staff (Coopee, 2000; Gaskin, 2000; Gillmore and Angus, 1999a). The end user needs only a standard Web browser and an e-mail client.

Using QuickPlace, nontechnical users can create and customize a self-administered, password-protected Web site on the fly, in less than one minute. Faculty and students can create discussion groups, develop Internet slide shows, host real-time conferences, develop a project plan using a group calendar and a Gantt chart,[8] download or upload documents by dragging their mouse across the desktop, or directly edit and track revisions of any Microsoft Office '97 or 2000 document posted to the site. Because each site is automatically assigned its own e-mail address, instructors and students can e-mail updates directly to it. In addition, students can receive regular newsletters from the site (on a daily or weekly basis), alerting them to new material or special announcements.

Over the next few years, there will likely be a proliferation of collaboration tools such as QuickPlace, so each institution must come to its own decision about which software package best suits its own needs. In particular, institutions should monitor the progress of an interesting peer-to-peer collaboration tool that has just been released, named Groove (www.groove.net), developed by Ray Ozzie, the creator of Lotus Notes (Alwang, 2001, McDougall, 2000, Scannell and Harreld, 2001). Although it is not my intention to promote any particular software package, I selected QuickPlace to develop the knowledge room concept for four reasons.

First, QuickPlace is based on the same proven architecture as Lotus Notes—an application widely viewed as the leading collaboration tool for large corporations. The benefit of QuickPlace is that it retains most of the collaborative functions of Lotus Notes without the administrative overhead of the Notes or Domino environment. This is no small benefit. Institutions of higher education must compete with corporations and government agencies to secure needed technical staff. Based on the current and expected demand for computer professionals in the corporate and government sectors, most institutions of higher education will find themselves at a disadvantage in their quest for technical personnel.

Second, QuickPlace is a software package built primarily for collaboration in a corporate setting and is not designed exclusively for educational institutions (although its customization features make this adaptation easy). It may seem odd to consider this an asset, but it is a very important point. Learning experiences in higher education should be as close to real life as possible. This is particularly important today, with the skill sets demanded by the information-based New Economy. Only a handful of students will ever use Blackboard, WebCT, or some other dedicated e-learning package following graduation. But teamware applications such as QuickPlace will likely be ubiquitous fixtures in the workplace. General Electric, for example, will be using QuickPlace as one of the key components of a companywide collaboration project among its 340,000 employees (Drucker, 2000). In addition, Lotus and IBM's next-generation knowledge management application, consisting of the K-station portal and the Discovery Server, has incorporated QuickPlace directly into the application (Copeland, 2001; Heck, 2001).

It only makes sense to educate students with the tools they are likely to use in the workplace.

Third, QuickPlace is currently the least expensive teamware product when compared with others that offer a similar range of features. At the time of this writing, QuickPlace 2.0 costs $39 per user per year for corporations and just $17 per user per year for academic institutions (with no additional fees per installed server). If schools purchase two-year licenses, the cost per year goes down to $10.50 per student! By comparison, eRoom 5.0 from eRoom Technology, Inc., a teamware application similar to QuickPlace, is priced at $9,995 per server and $199 per user.[9]

Finally, QuickPlace currently supports fifteen languages, including French, German, Spanish, Japanese, Korean, and simplified Chinese, and the list is likely to grow over the next few years. The fact that QuickPlace can be easily installed and administered locally makes it particularly attractive internationally because the application does not need to be run across heavily trafficked overseas Internet connections. Moreover, the off-line capability of QuickPlace makes the application well suited for intermittent or slower Internet connections.

Let us now take a brief look at each of the knowledge room types. Chapter Three will outline each one in detail, and Chapter Four will discuss some of the infrastructure issues associated with depth education.

The Research Center

The Research Center is a place of inquiry and discovery where students can develop skills in research and critical thinking. Each Research Center is built around a specific problem related to the course material (for example, applying a particular field of knowledge to the real world, a point of controversy in an academic discipline, a social dilemma that emerges as a result of new knowledge). A course may feature any number of Research Centers, with the proviso that each one be designed to accommodate groups of three to six students.

Because it is structured around the model of virtual teams (see Lipnack and Stamps, 1997), the Research Center becomes a primary vehicle for the formation of communities of inquiry and functions like a developmental incubator for skills in problem solving, planning, and communication. Moreover, because students are assigned a project leadership role on a rotating basis, it is a place where individual leadership skills can be nurtured. These skills not only are foundational for the New Economy but also prepare students for educational programs that they may pursue later in their careers.

Above all, the Research Center gets students used to a lifestyle of active learning in which education is a process of discovery, challenge, and inquiry—not absorption and recall. The significance of this, from a pedagogical standpoint, cannot be overstated. Much of the content that is currently delivered in the form of lectures can be readily incorporated as part of a resource library that is built into each Research Center, along with other materials (for example, articles, book excerpts, and guest lectures). Because students must use these materials to respond to a particular problem, content that was previously imprisoned in the lecture format can be liberated as a knowledge asset for research.

It is likely that liberal arts courses in the humanities and social sciences will make extensive use of Research Centers because of the more interpretative and expansive nature of these disciplines.

The Skill Workplace

The Skill Workplace provides students with the opportunity to acquire and practice a set of integral skills that are necessary to grasp a knowledge domain and complete the course successfully. Because these skills are discipline-specific and provide the foundation necessary for acquiring further knowledge in the discipline, the Skill Workplace is required of all students (although a fully articulated curriculum would be well served by a menu of specialized skill areas from which students could select). Each workplace includes an Office, which houses all the content resources for a particular skill (for example, lectures, textbook excerpts, articles, narrated PowerPoint presentations), and a suite of Exercise Rooms, designed for skill development and practice, which are assigned to each virtual team in the class. Only that group of students assigned to an Exercise Room may gain access to it. In addition, each Skill Workplace includes a help desk for peer-to-peer support (under the supervision of the instructor) and a skill gallery that gives the instructor the opportunity to spotlight exceptional work by specific virtual teams. Both the help desk and the skill gallery reinforce a key insight of the New Economy— it is important to take advantage of every opportunity to learn from one's peers. Developing a culture that supports knowledge sharing is just as important for educational institutions as it is for technologically advanced corporations competing in the global marketplace.

One important issue associated with the Skill Workplace is how to define integral skills for a particular discipline. Often the term *skill* is taken to mean the application of a particular piece of knowledge toward some practical end—in effect, conjuring up a skill for every parcel of knowledge learned. Much of the blame for the trivialization of skills should be laid at the doorstep of the behaviorist tradition in education. Behavioral psychology, when translated into the classroom, encourages teachers to segment learning into bite-size, discrete components that are often taught in isolation from one another (Walker and Lambert, 1995). With few exceptions, students are rarely given the opportunity to practice bringing these components together outside of contrived, made-to-order, textbook situations.

The effect of this is to diminish the integrative and empowering dimensions of the skill concept. Although certainly any skill relies on a baseline threshold of knowledge, a skill is something that empowers the learner to unlock new knowledge vistas; it is not an ad hoc collection of applied knowledge nuggets. Integral skills are basic proficiencies for working in a discipline—relating to its core concepts and methodologies. Defining such basic skills is no easy task. It can only be done on a course-specific basis for each discipline. More will be said about this in Chapter Four in relation to the knowledge management matrix.

Presumably, a course in organic chemistry or finance would be strongly weighted toward more Skill Workplaces than the other knowledge room components, given the pronounced investment that students must make in learning the methods of these disciplines.

The Conference Center

The Conference Center can be thought of as a kind of incubator for the development of critical thinking skills and the formation of communities of inquiry. The Conference Center features a suite of Seminar Rooms and builds on the tried-and-true success of the seminar format.

Each Seminar Room is devoted to a specific topic. Although some instructors may wish to run these seminars concurrently, normally they would be held in a predefined sequence that dovetails with the unfolding themes of the course. In addition, students can be given the opportunity to develop and facilitate their own seminars on topics of interest throughout the course—either for extra credit or as part of the course assignments.

The primary benefit of the seminar format is that it gives students the opportunity to develop the habit of inquiry and extend their skills in critical thinking. Although these seminars do not rely on the preparation, presentation, and critique of student papers, as in traditional graduate seminars, they do require a *content centerpiece* for the discussion. This content centerpiece may be a case study, article, student paper, lecture, video clip, or book excerpt—anything that brings focus to the discussion and stimulates reflection and critical appraisal. Thus, these seminars are not simply free-form discussion strings built on stream-of-consciousness responses. They are focused opportunities for exploration and critique that replicate something of the roundtable ethos of the graduate seminar.

Because each Conference Center—and the seminar discussions contained in it—can be archived for future use, it is possible over time to build a rich repertoire of discussion material that could be reviewed and critiqued by future students.

This introduces some interesting possibilities for incorporating a kind of intergenerational aspect to the knowledge room structure, as students can benefit from the contributions of previous generations of students. For example, a professor could make a point of recycling a few standard seminar topics each time the course is taught. When the class has completed one of these standard discussions, the professor could give students access to an archived seminar held by a previous class. The current class would then be asked to compare their own performance to the archived discussion, noting, for instance, particular strengths or weaknesses in critical thinking or how each class developed different themes or approaches to the material. This process exposes students to a wider range of thinking and a richer idea environment than would be possible in a onetime seminar discussion.

This intergenerational potential of the Conference Center could be developed further if there are also guest respondents, particularly alumni, in connection with specific seminar topics. Because of the common association between academic community and the physical college campus, it is tacitly assumed that when one departs from the college campus, one leaves an academic community. This makes no sense in the Internet age. We need a broader definition of instructional faculty that incorporates the important contributions of alumni and retired professionals (see Hamilton, 2001). Why not have volunteer coeducators serve alongside faculty members? Depending on their interest and expertise, these volunteer coeducators could serve alongside faculty in specific segments of the course.

Indeed, a key strength of e-learning is its ability to leverage the knowledge assets of alumni and retired professionals for the benefit of students. With the continuing trend of people living longer and using their retirement years to explore alternate careers and avenues of service, educational institutions would really be remiss if they did not exploit this opportunity. Individuals who agreed to serve in this capacity could be e-mailed when a seminar discussion that matches their own interests and expertise will take place. This not only would bring a great wealth of knowledge and experience to the classroom but also would enhance the diversity and "reflective capacity" of individual communities of inquiry.

The Debate Hall

The Debate Hall is a virtual environment where students can participate in a formal debate (hosted in an asynchronous or an "anytime, anywhere" format) and benefit from constructive criticism from other members of the class. Like a traditional debate, each virtual debate is structured around a debate proposition and features both initial presentations and rebuttals by the affirmative and negative teams.

Educators who already incorporate formal classroom debates in their courses are well aware of how they can enliven class discussions and underscore the relevance of course content. One of the virtues of the debate structure is that the teams on both sides of the issue must be conversant with the evidence and arguments that support the opposing position. Debates also highlight important points of internal dissent in a particular discipline, focusing on how a different set of assumptions and methodologies can produce dramatically different conclusions. This moves students away from the homogenous orientation of textbook-based surface learning toward an in-depth understanding of a discipline and its own particular set of conceptual dilemmas and methodological problems.

It may seem odd or counterproductive to hold debates in an anytime, anywhere virtual environment, if you think about how real-time debates lend considerable energy to classroom interactions. Yet three factors argue in favor of virtual debates.

First, a virtual debate places the emphasis squarely on content—exactly where it should be. It is often quite difficult to evaluate live debates strictly on the merits of content, particularly when students have either exceptionally strong or weak presentation skills. Matters of style invariably affect the degree to which a position is perceived as compelling and coherent. This fact is not lost on the conscientious student who prepares carefully for a debate yet worries that much of his or her hard work will go unnoticed if the oral presentation is weak. Although the development of oral presentation skills is an important curricular outcome for higher education, the ability to write a persuasive and compelling argument is equally important. In fact, one could argue that a well-written memo often carries more weight than a memorable presentation in many organizational settings.

Second, much material that could be included in a written argument, particularly sources, cannot be easily included in an oral argument. Although instructors can always collect and evaluate the debate notes of each team, this is an immensely time-consuming process that leaves the rest of the class out of the loop when it comes to their evaluation of the debate. Also, one can more fully assimilate and reflect on a written argument than an oral argument, as with legal briefs submitted in advance of court proceedings, because one can reread and reevaluate the argument without the distractions of the classroom environment or the pressure of completing a debate evaluation. This is particularly useful in encouraging high-quality debate evaluations from each of the students.

Third, instructors can structure more debates in a course than would be possible with in-class debates alone simply because of the time involved. Because all students in the class have the benefit of viewing and evaluating each debate, a rich range of disciplinary issue areas can be addressed during a single course. Moreover, collaboration in a virtual environment is easier because each debate team has its own document repository, group calendar, and task assignment facility. These features, along with the ability to set up a real-time conference and to edit a presentation cooperatively, allow students to collaborate on debate preparations more efficiently.

The Portfolio Gallery

The Portfolio Gallery is a knowledge room devoted to creative expression and project presentation. Students, working either individually or with one or two other students, can use the Portfolio Gallery to exhibit their work and receive reviews from their student colleagues, which are e-mailed directly to the site (see Lange, 2000). In effect, this enables students to develop their own secure Web site for a single project, or perhaps, a constellation of course assignments. Because the emphasis of the Portfolio Gallery is on creativity, students are encouraged to customize the look and feel of their site, organizing material as they see fit. The exceptionally intuitive structure of QuickPlace makes it possible for students to build an elaborate on-line portfolio with little instruction from the faculty member.

One of the signal benefits of the Portfolio Gallery is that it can serve as a vehicle for multicourse integration in a particular program or department or as a device for interdisciplinary "capstone" work in a liberal arts setting. Furthermore, there is no reason why a portfolio must remain active only during a student's tenure. Ideally, it could become an important resume-building resource for a graduate's ongoing career development. This aspect of the Portfolio Gallery will be discussed in Chapter Five.

Depth Education: A "Bricks-and-Clicks" Model

Depth education is a hybrid or blended approach to e-learning that combines the best features of the brick-and-mortar classroom with virtual environments. In contrast to approaches that use e-learning technologies as another delivery system for traditional education, depth education can be implemented in a holistic fashion across the disciplinary span of college and university curricula, thereby placing e-learning at the core of the curriculum.

A distinct advantage of the knowledge room approach is that educators can contextualize and control the extent to which knowledge rooms are integrated in the classroom experience. This not only facilitates a graduated approach to technology integration but also, more importantly, promotes the development of an ethos of classroom experimentation. There is no sense that one must leap off a cliff with the knowledge room concept. A minimalist implementation of knowledge rooms—deploying, for example, a Conference Center or a few Research Centers in a course—will lay a foundation for more extensive integration in subsequent semesters.

Although depth education involves additional costs associated with the campus library, faculty development, technical support, and network capacity, the knowledge room model has the potential to reduce costs in other areas—savings primarily associated with the more intensive use of classroom space. Depending on the configuration selected by the institution or instructor, students would need to meet in a physical classroom only 25 to 33 percent of the time normally spent on traditional classroom-based instruction (for example, one hour a week for a three-credit course). The effect of this would be to increase existing classroom capacity by 200 to 300 percent without building any additional classrooms (see Bleed, 2001; Carnevale, 1999a). Furthermore, depth education does not require schools to build expensive high-tech classrooms.

In the lingo of e-commerce, depth education is built on a *clicks-and-mortar* or *bricks-and-clicks* model. With the demise of so many dot-com firms following the precipitous fall of the NASDAQ in April 2000, there is growing recognition of the inherent limitations of enterprises that have only a virtual existence. Amazon.com, for example, has survived in an increasingly competitive marketplace by developing a large brick-and-mortar distribution network. E*Trade, the immensely successful on-line brokerage firm, one of the few to prosper from advertising during Super Bowl 2000 and make a return engagement for Super Bowl 2001, has now adopted a bricks-and-clicks strategy by beginning to establish physical branch offices (Forster, 2001).

There are indications that a bricks-and-clicks orientation to e-learning—one that does not accept the either-or dichotomy between classroom-based and distance education—is beginning to take shape. Such evidence comes from recent developments in the arenas of both corporate training and higher education.

For example, a white paper from International Data Corporation (2000a) entitled "eLearning in Practice: Blended Solutions in Action" concludes that a blended solution consisting of live training and "self-paced training and technology delivery offers an effective, convenient and flexible solution to a wide range of training needs" (p. 13).[10] Countrywide Home Loans, ExecuTrain, Ford, and Intel have already put such blended solutions into practice (International Data Corporation, 2000b; McGee, 2001; Swanson, 2001).

In higher education, Carnegie Mellon University is on the leading edge of using technology to enhance classroom-based learning. Students, enjoying the benefits of a wireless campus network, use a collaboration application known as TeamCMU to work on class projects with other students at all hours of the day or night (Hamm, 2000). Traditional liberal arts schools are also taking steps to infuse technology into their curricula. For example, Wake Forest University is providing its faculty and students with Macromedia's Dreamweaver, one of the industry's premiere Web-authoring applications, and providing training in how to use it ("Students Weave," 1999).

Another promising instance of using the Internet to add richness to the curriculum was described at the Summit on Technology in Liberal Arts Colleges, held at Middlebury College in June 2000. Thirteen out of fifteen institutions in the Associated Colleges of the South have formed a virtual classics department—one of the largest classics departments in the United States. Their first course—Advanced Latin—was offered in fall 2000. The course, team-taught by six professors, is being implemented in the following manner:

> At the appointed time, the professors and about 30 students—a few from each of the six campuses—will tune in to an on-line audio broadcast of a lecture. During the lecture, they can pose questions and make comments in a live chat room. The six professors will take turns lecturing each week. To supplement the on-line lectures, students from each campus will meet for a second time each week in a tutorial session with their own professor; those sessions are scheduled at different times on different campuses. All of the students and professors will also participate in an ongoing on-line discussion. [Young, 2000d, p. 34]

The purpose of such a blended approach is not to boost course enrollments or economize on faculty resources but rather to enhance the quality of education.

Perhaps the most notable example of a blended solution for higher education comes from the Wharton School at the University of Pennsylvania. Beginning with a pilot program during fall 1998, Wharton was an early pioneer of a bricks-and-clicks approach to e-learning. Instead of using the Internet as a tool for delivery of course content, the faculty and administration wanted a collaboration tool that would facilitate group work on course projects outside the classroom as well as promote better communication with teachers. Toward this end, Wharton selected a proven collaboration tool, eRoom, instead of using an application designed specifically for education. The school went about the task of adapting eRoom to its undergraduate and graduate programs. The result was webCafé.

WebCafé has been an unqualified success. During the fall 1998 pilot program, it was rolled out to five classroom-based courses. By spring 1999, it was integrated into twenty-one courses. A year later, in the spring 2000 semester, the number of courses that used webCafé increased to fifty-three. By fall 2000, that number reached sixty. When one factors in Wharton's executive education seminars, more than ninety courses have integrated webCafé into their classes (Agnew, 2000; Drucker, 1999; Rob Ditto, e-mail correspondence with the author, July and October 2000). Anne Greenhalgh, codirector of Wharton's undergraduate Management 100 course, and associate professor of management, describes webCafé as the place "where the lecture hall, the boardroom, and the student café converge. As a virtual meeting place for teams, it offers busy people a great opportunity to make team decisions and continue progress on important projects. From an academic standpoint, webCafé provides a new avenue of exchange outside of the class meeting times. It lessens the barriers between teacher and student, facilitates peer advising and strengthens the community" ("Wharton's Undergrads," 1999).

Wharton's blended approach to e-learning reveals a key insight about the Internet: interaction across time can be just as important as or more important than interaction across distance. Using digital technologies to add dimensionality to face-to-face communities is likely to be considerably more successful than trying to create digital communities from scratch. For this reason, as Brown and Duguid (2000, pp. 226) note, "Technologies may do a better job on the conventional campus than on the virtual one." Given the success of webCafé in their curriculum, Wharton is marketing its adaptation of eRoom as part of a service to other educational institutions ("Wharton Earns an ASP Degree," 1999; Berinato, 2000).

Discovery, Discernment, and the Classroom

Discovery and discernment are cornerstone skills for the New Economy. The Old Economy, with its assembly line mentality, placed a premium on absorbing information and recalling it. This approach has been rendered obsolete by the explosion of information and the dynamic behavior of networks. Accordingly, classrooms should no longer serve as information depots, where lectures are stacked ready for delivery on the loading dock and exams function as little more than signed bills of lading.

Depth education frees up space in the classroom for the important work of stimulating intellectual curiosity and fostering critical thinking skills. One day, perhaps in the not-too-distant future, it may be possible to dispense entirely with the face-to-face classroom. That will depend on how compelling the videoconferencing applications of the next-generation Internet (or Internet2) will be. In the meantime, two vital ingredients of physical classroom environments will be very difficult to duplicate in virtual space. The first is a teacher's passion for intellectual inquiry and love for his or her subject. The second is the unique chemistry of each class. Both qualities are best experienced in real time (see Traub, 2000).

Good classes and good theater have much in common. Just as the audience's composition and demeanor influence a live dramatic presentation, every teacher knows that each class is unique. The same material evokes different responses from one class to the next. Body language, voice intonation, the way questions are asked, the classroom setting, the responses of others—all of these factors affect the student's learning experience.

In the model of depth education, the purpose of classroom meetings will necessarily vary from course to course. For example, much of the time allocated for face-to-face interactions in science courses would likely be devoted to labs. Courses in the humanities and social sciences might use a portion of class time for student presentations, role-play exercises, impromptu case studies, guest speakers, or field trips. Certainly some portion of each class should be devoted to reflective discussion about the students' interactions in each of the course knowledge rooms.

Also, the geographic flexibility made possible by e-learning can be used to good advantage when it comes to providing students with discovery-laden experiences. For example, colleges and universities could incorporate a wide spectrum of cross-cultural experiences and ecotourism in their curricula. There is no compelling reason why, for example, college classes could not be held in national parks or exotic venues around the world, particularly because faculty members would not have to be physically present (although they may wish to be). Dormitories and classroom buildings have their limitations—even on the quaintest of college campuses. One fine example of how such geographical flexibility can add richness to a curriculum comes from the master's degree program in conflict analysis and management at Royal Roads University in Victoria, British Columbia. This two-year distance education program features weeklong missions to Bosnia and the United Nations in New York City. Students use this opportunity to do firsthand research on peacekeeping (Paskey, 2000).

The Academy and Technological Resistance

Depth education will fall flat on its face if one factor is missing—a spirit of experimentation in the classroom. Neither the mix-and-match flexibility of the knowledge room concept nor the intuitive design of teamware applications like QuickPlace will be of much value if the old ways of teaching, which have served faculty so well, reign supreme.

Tradition is a core value for most academics—and for good reason. Of all contemporary social institutions, colleges and universities are the most enduring. As Clark Kerr (1995, p. 115) notes:

> About eighty-five institutions in the Western world established by 1520 still
> exist in recognizable forms, with similar functions and with unbroken histories,
> including the Catholic Church, the Parliaments of the Isle of Man, of Iceland,
> and of Great Britain, several Swiss cantons, and seventy universities. Kings that

rule, feudal lords with vassals, and guilds with monopolies are all gone. These seventy universities, however, are still in the same locations with some of the same buildings, with professors and students doing much the same things, and with governance carried on in much the same ways. There have been many intervening variations on ancient themes, it is true, but the eternal themes of teaching, scholarship, and service, in one combination or another, continue.

The aura of institutional resilience surrounding higher education is strengthened by the fact that the colleges and universities have been exceptionally successful in providing venues for transformation and growth for generations of young people. Educators have the privilege of personally witnessing this growth and transformation with the passing of each academic year. It is no wonder that many would resist the introduction (or, worse yet, imposition) of some new learning technology or method that will allegedly "revolutionize" the classroom experience.[11] The potential success of e-learning in higher education has been seriously impeded by overeager vendors who overstate the benefits of the latest technology or overzealous administrators who—with dollar signs in their eyes—have suspended their disbelief (see Feenberg, 1999).

The title of a recent book on computer-mediated education nicely captures the sentiment shared by many academics when it comes to technology and the classroom—*Dancing with the Devil*. Although the authors of the book (Katz and Associates, 1999) are decidedly upbeat about the prospects of computer-mediated education, they harbor no illusions that it will be anything but an uphill struggle. Some may suspect that faculty resistance to new technologies is much like a repeat performance of the medieval crafts guilds' resistance to the technological developments that launched the Industrial Revolution.

Yet such resistance is more likely to come from pragmatists than closet Luddites. There are striking parallels, for example, between the extravagant enthusiasm associated with the classroom use of instructional television during the 1960s (some proponents predicted that 50 percent of each college class would be occupied by viewing instructional television) and the current hype about distance education (Neal, 1998). Good teachers—not technological tools—open up new worlds for students.

A basic fact of life in academia is that nothing will change unless faculty are behind it. As A. W. Bates (2000, p. 95) emphasizes, "Presidents may dream visions, and vice presidents may design plans, and deans and department heads may try to implement them, but without the support of faculty members nothing will change." Ultimately, change will come if e-learning provides a demonstrable improvement in the academic quality of life for both students and faculty. The virtue of depth education in this regard is that it approaches e-learning as a process initiated "from below." Programs that are mandated on a top-down basis or segregated in separate (but rarely equal) institutional units will be inevitably pushed to the fringes of campus life, serving no one well. Students deserve much more than this.

Certainly, fear is the most formidable barrier to change (Bates, 2000). Although administrators may be tempted to chalk faculty fears up to a generalized fear of change, they should not dismiss these concerns in this manner. The fact is that there are objective grounds for concern about the institution of tenure, the disconnect between faculty efforts to improve teaching and the rewards structure for professional advancement, the growing prominence of part-time faculty, and the long-term economic viability of many academic institutions. Such fears are not figments of the imagination; it is dishonest to maintain that they are.

Yet no real progress can be made if fear occupies a place of prominence in academic life. Fear paralyzes imagination, raises suspicions, and shuts down opportunities. Strong academic leadership can make the difference here—addressing, not dismissing, such concerns by bringing them into the light of day.

CHAPTER TWO

THE COMMODITIZATION OF INSTRUCTION

The following conversation between an Italian farmer and his granddaughter, taken from an IBM advertisement, is familiar to most of us:

Grandfather: Well, I finally finished my doctoral thesis.
Young woman: Way to go, Gramps!
Grandfather: Did my research at Indiana University.
Young woman: Indiana?
Grandfather: Yup. IBM took the school's library . . . and digitized it. So I could access it over the Internet. . . . You know. . . . It's a great time to be alive. [Brown and Duguid, 2000, p. 207]

Although the alleged facts in this heartwarming exchange are fictitious (IBM helped digitize only a portion of the music collection at Indiana University, not the entire library), the advertisement is as revealing as a Rorschach inkblot on our attitudes about e-learning and higher education (Brown and Duguid, 2000). Even if the entire collection of Indiana University were digitized in our lifetime—frankly, an unlikely prospect—there is a lot more to Ph.D. programs than gaining digital access to a library. The ad is a striking example of our low expectations for higher education—that the lowest common denominator of educational experiences, the information transaction, is often seen as the defining feature of learning.

The assumption that e-learning is more about distance than depth betrays a bias of reach over richness. The effect of this bias is to make e-learning captive to distance education. There is perhaps no more eloquent testimony to this bias than the "no significant difference" literature. This body of research, including over four hundred studies, examines the overall effectiveness of distance education (including interactive Web courses and courses that make use of videos or conventional printed materials) compared with the classroom delivery system of traditional education.

According to Thomas L. Russell, director emeritus of instructional telecommunications at North Carolina State University, there is no significant difference between distance education techniques and traditional approaches (see http://teleeducation.nb.ca/nosignificantdifference/). He claims that "all delivery mechanisms—be they simple print or sophisticated computer-based or interactive video-based—had a like result" (Young, 2000b, p. A55). Other reviews of these data have raised questions about the methodological shortcomings of many of these studies (Blumenstyk and McCollum, 1999; Merisotis and Phipps, 1999; Lockee, Moore, and Burton, 2001).

Irrespective of one's judgment of the methodological problems of this literature, the significant thing about the "no significant difference" literature is that the research question has been deemed significant in the first place. Why should one hold up lecture-based classroom education as the benchmark for evaluating new educational delivery systems? If there is no significant difference between distance education and classroom education, advocates of distance education should not trumpet this claim; they should be troubled by it. Taken as a whole, the "no significant difference" literature may represent the most egregious application of benchmarking in the past twenty years. The status quo becomes the standard for evaluating learning technologies that have much more to offer.

Proponents of distance education will likely object to the characterization that there is no additional benefit with distance learning, asserting that Internet-based instruction involves a higher degree of student interaction than possible in the traditional classroom—particularly among students who are less apt to speak up in the classroom. This is a legitimate point. Yet, if a student's participation in on-line or face-to-face discussions is so important, why have distance learning advocates casually accepted the either-or thinking between distance learning and face-to-face classroom interaction? One either teaches in a brick-and-mortar classroom or teaches at a distance in a virtual classroom. Why not a hybrid or blended approach that combines the best of e-learning and classroom-based interaction? Given that most distance education courses draw primarily *on-campus* students, because of conflicts with work schedules and other classes (Guernsey,

1998a; University of Illinois Faculty Seminar, 1999), the persistence of such either-or thinking is nothing short of breathtaking.

Distance Education as Deus Ex Machina

A lot of the enthusiasm for distance education stems from the hope that Web-based instruction will enable colleges and universities to serve more students with less—in much the same way as the device used in Greek tragedies rescued the protagonist from irresolvable dilemmas. Senior administrators and board members have viewed distance education as a way to accommodate projected increases in student enrollment without building more parking lots, dormitories, and classrooms.

There has been no shortage of commercial enterprises responding to this market opportunity. Distance education facilitators such as Blackboard (www.blackboard.com), the Caliber Learning Network (www.caliber.com), Campus Pipeline (www.campuspipeline.com), Convene (www.convene.com), eCollege.com (formerly Real Education), the Global Education Network (www.gen.com), University Access (www.universityaccess.com), WebCT.com (www.webct.com), and WBT Systems (www.wbtsystems.com) have positioned themselves to serve this market (see Block and Dobell, 1999). Even Columbia University, Cornell University, Duke University, New York University, Temple University, and the University of Maryland have all taken the step of forming for-profit subsidiaries to market their distance education courses (Carr, 1999b, 2000e, 2000h; Carnevale, 1999b; "Duke Business-School Venture," 2000).

Perhaps the most notable entrant in this field is UNext.com, an e-learning initiative headquartered in Deerfield, Illinois, that has partnered with Carnegie Mellon University, Columbia University, the London School of Economics and Political Science, Stanford University, and the University of Chicago. Founded by Andy Rosenfield, an educator and entrepreneur in his late forties, UNext.com is investing up to $1 million per course to develop a high-quality Internet curriculum that uses problem-based learning. Backed by investors like financier Michael Milken and Larry Ellison of the Oracle Corporation, UNext.com has formed its own degree-granting institution—Cardean University—named after the Roman goddess who guarded doorways (or Internet portals?). By 2001, they plan to have about one hundred courses on-line. Over the long term, UNext.com's Cardean University envisions a student body in the millions (Carr, 2000b; McCormick, 2000).

Textbook publishers and educational service providers have also entered the distance education marketplace. For example, McGraw-Hill (www.mhla.net) has created partnerships with Blackboard and WebCT to facilitate the use of its course texts in distance learning environments. Harcourt General even opened a for-profit university named Harcourt Higher Education (Blumenstyk, 1999, 2000a). In August 2000, the Massachusetts Board of Higher Education licensed its degree programs. After enrolling only thirty-two paying students, the new owner of Harcourt, the Thomson Corporation, decided to close down the on-line college in September 2001 (Blumenstyk, 2001d).

The Case for Sobriety

In the string of dot-com failures that have occurred since the precipitous fall of the NASDAQ in April 2000, it is now clear that good judgment was the first casualty of the Internet age. The dot-com frenzy that drove up stock values and promised to redefine the commercial landscape has evaporated before the hard realities of the marketplace. The traditional virtues of stability and profitability now seem less mundane in relation to market share and "first-mover" advantage. The new rule of the information superhighway is that decision making and digital euphoria do not mix.

The roster of once-promising but now-collapsed Internet firms grows longer each day. Many others remain in intensive care or have been forced into successively brutal rounds of downsizing. The contrast between the ads during Super Bowl 2000 and 2001 could not have been more striking. Even the future of well-branded, pioneering Internet companies such as Priceline.com, the "name your own price" firm, remains in doubt (Angwin, 2001). Key executives have fled, and Priceline's stock has fluctuated between $1.30 and $9.10 a share in the first half of 2001 (it was $104 a share in mid-March 2000).

Of the many accounts of dot-com misfortunes, the story of Living.com, a furniture e-tailer, is particularly poignant. For nearly sixty years, the Shaw Furniture Gallery was a vital brick-and-mortar business, employing sixty-five people from the vicinity of High Point, North Carolina. Then Shaw decided to partner with a high-flying Internet firm, Living.com, a company with billion-dollar revenue projections that was mentioned in the same breath as Amazon.com. Living.com promised to make Shaw part of the biggest furniture outlet the world has ever known. On August 29, 2000, Living.com declared bankruptcy and brought down Shaw Furniture Gallery with it (Richtel, 2000).

One hopes that institutions of higher education will benefit from the lessons of the once high-flying dot-com firms that have fallen back to earth. Thankfully, there is a growing recognition that distance education will not be a financial windfall for colleges and universities (Hawkins, 2000). In fact, some appear to be losing money from their distance education initiatives (Carr, 2001a). Pensare, the company that worked closely with Duke University's on-line MBA Programs, has recently filed for bankruptcy and is going out of business (Blumenstyk, 2001b). Temple University has shut down its for-profit distance education company (Blumenstyk, 2001c), and even the well-funded UNext is struggling in the face of a weak distance education market (Carr, 2001c). Much of the technological hype and the general early enthusiasm for distance education have now been replaced with skepticism.

It is tempting to dismiss Internet-based distance education as a holdover from the dot-com frenzy of the late 1990s. Yet it would be a serious mistake to do so. If it were not for the broadband virtual classroom, made possible by the growth of residential broadband Internet, one could perhaps view distance education as a flash-in-the-pan, an ivory tower equivalent of IPO mania.

One of the more spectacular miscalculations of the past two or three years has been the overproduction of extensive fiber optic backbones without enough attention being paid to the "last-mile" connections to homes and businesses. This has cost telecommunications firms billions and virtually guarantees that millions of miles of optical fiber will not be "lit" for years to come (Blumenstein, 2001, Romero, 2001). In the meantime, a typical residential broadband connection of 600 kilobits per second (which translates to an average speed of 300 to 500 kilobits per second, due to bottlenecks in Internet transmission) is insufficient for high-quality video feeds and videoconferencing (Brown, 2001). It may be a decade or more before local digital networks can support true broadband connection speeds in the one to three megabits per second range. One seasoned observer, reflecting on the resilience of computer standards (like the narrowband Internet standard of 34 kilobits per second) once they are in place, has lamented that it may be decades before residential broadband is commonplace (Dvorak, 2001). Lest one is inclined to dismiss such a statement as hyperbole, one should remember that it is only with the release of Windows XP operating system, scheduled for the fourth quarter of 2001, that Microsoft has purged its archaic DOS platform from its consumer line.

Given these qualifications, once residential broadband in the one to three megabits per second range is widespread, it will be possible to create a virtual classroom that could accommodate seven hundred to two thousand students. All of these students will be able to see and hear the instructor, view PowerPoint slides, respond to survey questions posed by the instructor and view the results of each poll immediately, and send questions to a help desk, where they will be answered by a battery of content experts. Most of these features are already built into standard virtual classroom packages like the LearningSpace Collaboration Module from Lotus and IBM or Conference Center 2000 from PlaceWare. In addition, students who need to review a specific point of the lecture will be able to do so by means of a playback feature. A team of teaching assistants will be able to handle all the discussion sections and grading for the class.

It will be difficult to argue on pedagogical grounds for the superiority of the traditional lecture hall over the broadband virtual classroom. A broadband virtual classroom with a thousand students could be considerably more interactive than a traditional lecture with just fifty. It will also render obsolete the standard post-a-lecture and host-a-discussion e-learning model of distance education. Any inconvenience associated with needing to be in front of a computer screen at a designated time will be more than compensated for by the feeling of not being alone and the reassurance of seeing a professor holding forth in the classroom. The broadband virtual classroom will be able to replicate enough of the look and feel of the large lecture hall to reassure both students and parents that they are not getting a second-rate education.

The relevance of distance education for working professionals also should not be discounted. The growth of the on-line programs at the University of Phoenix has been nothing short of remarkable. Between May 31, 1999 and May 31, 2000, the university's on-line program grew by 44.7 percent to include 13,779 students. Enrollment in the university's on-line courses has doubled since 1998 ("University of Phoenix Reports," 2000).

Commoditization as a Long-Term Trend

Higher education's flirtation with distance education is indicative of a more pervasive trend evident for some time in academia—the commoditization of instruction (Noble, 1998a). *Commoditization* refers to the process whereby products or services become so standardized that their attributes are roughly the same. Things that were once apples and oranges become apples and apples. When a product or service is commoditized, it can be readily compared with other products like it, and competition revolves strictly around price. Agricultural commodities are the classic case. Grain standards, which have evolved over five thousand years, have become sophisticated measures for comparability. For instance, No. 1 amber durum wheat is a sufficiently standardized measure that it can be marketed globally based on price, no matter which country of origin or particular producer.

The commoditization of instruction is evident on nearly all college and university campuses. This process has been greatly facilitated by two factors: a minimalist definition of education that focuses on information transfer, and the widespread use of adjunct faculty to reduce the cost of instruction. Textbook producers, standardized exams, the increased use of transfer credit, and the tendency among faculty to understand their teaching responsibilities as "covering the material" have further reinforced this trend. Students have also done their fair share to reinforce commoditization because it facilitates the strategic comparison of courses (with courses that require the least amount of time and hold the greatest promise for a good grade being favored).

The increased use of adjunct instructors instead of full-time faculty is obviously a hot-button issue in academia. The latest figures from the U.S. Department of Education, covering 1997, indicate that adjunct faculty make up nearly half the professoriate (42.5 percent), compared with 22 percent in 1970. Furthermore, part-time faculty made up over twice as many of the new hires when compared with full-time faculty (Leatherman, 2000). This is part of a continuing trend to reduce the costs of education by outsourcing teaching services at what may be called "bargain basement prices."

There is, of course, no reason why the teaching services of adjunct faculty should be seen as less valuable than those of full-time faculty. We would be in a much different situation if schools made an authentic investment in adjunct instructors—paying them what they are worth, encouraging their professional development, and safeguarding their academic freedom. But this is clearly not the case. The trend toward adjuncts is motivated by the raw economics of holding down instructional budgets. A recent survey found that part-time faculty are rarely afforded benefits and make less than $3,000 per course, even when teaching four courses per term. This puts adjunct faculty compensation on a par with that of porters and fast-food workers (Cox, 2000). As Zachary Karabell (1998, p. 193) writes, "Many adjuncts have Ph.D.'s, but they make less money than the people who clean the classrooms they teach in." One would expect that the wave of impending retirements of full-time faculty over this decade (see Magner, 2000) will provide new opportunities to replace full-time faculty with adjuncts.

The combined effects of overutilization and underinvestment with respect to adjunct faculty is self-defeating for all concerned. Not only has this created a class of "gypsy scholars" that serve educational institutions "without hope of permanence or authority" (O'Donnell, 1998, p. 180), but also it has reinforced the belief that the teaching services of full-time faculty can be readily outsourced without a corresponding decline in quality.

Remarkably, full-time faculty have been all too willing accomplices in this commoditization of instruction. Their silence is deafening when it comes to advocating on behalf of their part-time colleagues (Karabell, 1998). This complacent posture is all the more indefensible in light of the abrogation of academic freedom that is often tacitly understood to be one of the rules of the game in adjunct appointments. Adjuncts who create classroom controversy can be dropped in a moment on administrative whim (Schneider, 1999). This rarely creates a stir among their full-time counterparts. If academic freedom is such an important asset for higher education, how can tenured faculty remain indifferent to the fundamental vulnerability of their adjunct colleagues?

One suspects that a primary factor in the commoditization of instruction is a profound ambiguity that goes to the heart of faculty identity. Are faculty primarily researchers or teachers? Although the Boyer report (1990) recognized multiple expressions for scholarship, the reward system for most tenure-track faculty is strongly biased in favor of research. Effective teaching may often be recognized in the evaluation process but it is not nearly as important as being a productive scholar (that is, publishing articles in refereed journals). Consequently, faculty are encouraged to invest primarily in the learning communities specific to their disciplines (sustained by an endless ritual of professional conferences), instead of cultivating communities of inquiry on their own campuses. One distinguished political scientist at Harvard commented as follows: "I have more in common with scholars in my field who teach in Japan than I do with professors across the hall. I e-mail Japan several times a week, but I might not speak to colleagues in other disciplines more than a few times in a decade." (Karabell, 1998, p. 151).

The fact that research is rewarded in a way that teaching is not makes it rational to invest oneself only minimally in the classroom. Whatever the drawbacks of the lecture methodology from the standpoint of actual learning, it is a proven time-saver from the standpoint of faculty. Lecture materials can be easily recycled from one year to the next with little or no protest among students. More importantly, the lecture methodology makes it possible for schools to cram hundreds of students into a single class, maximizing the economic value of faculty time and using undercompensated graduate students to carry the heaviest burdens of leading discussion sections and grading.

Computer-Based Instruction and Commoditization

With this tacit approval for the commoditization of instruction among both faculty and administrators, it is no surprise that instructional technologies have been construed in a manner that facilitates it. The history of computer-based instruction is instructive in this regard.

Much of the fanfare over the use of computers in classroom settings in the late 1980s and throughout much of the 1990s centered on how they could perform instructional services to supplement or replace faculty. Two teaching functions in particular seemed to be excellent candidates for substituting the computer for faculty members: the delivery of information through lectures, and testing and evaluation.

Early in the development of computer-based instruction, simple DOS programs used an antiquated rote-learning methodology. They presented students with a sequence of information screens with accompanying self-tests based on that information (Jonassen, 1996). With the evolution of interactive multimedia authoring systems and CD-ROM technology, these "flat" DOS programs were replaced by considerably more sophisticated and layered programs. The concept of interactivity for most of these programs amounted to little more than a menu-driven interface that incorporated buttons, hot spots, and videos that could be stopped and reversed. These allowed students to proceed through the material at their own pace, repeating what was unclear and skipping topics they already knew about. The more sophisticated of these programs used quizzes and tests to direct students (if they scored poorly) to remedial instructional modules in the curriculum.

The value of such programs is obvious in the case of adult students, who enter the classroom from widely divergent backgrounds and have differing levels of knowledge or anxiety about the subject matter. Similarly, this approach is well suited to content that requires a considerable degree of repetitive practice for mastery, such as language studies. Nevertheless, the educational methodology behind these programs was essentially that of rote education, except that now students could focus on the topics they wished to master.[1]

For the most part, Web-based instruction has simply combined the computer-based instructional paradigm with the World Wide Web. All forms of Web-based instruction fall into two general categories: asynchronous instruction and synchronous instruction. The distinction is the method of delivery. Asynchronous instruction can take place at any time, from anywhere. Synchronous instruction requires the simultaneous participation of both teacher and students, but from any location.

The emerging consensus is that stand-alone degree programs that rely on Web-based instruction will need to combine elements of both asynchronous and synchronous instruction. Although asynchronous instruction is definitely more convenient for students, there is a greater risk of noncompletion and feelings of isolation associated with such programs. Having a scheduled class time and being able to have questions answered immediately (through electronic "hand-raising" functions built into virtual classroom packages) will likely be a significant benefit for most students. The downside of synchronous instructional formats, besides potential scheduling difficulties, is that they require either two phone lines (one for a telephone conference call and the other for a standard Internet connection) or a fast and dependable broadband Internet connection.

It is worth noting that the synchronous format for Web-based instruction reverses the trend of trying to use computer technology to substitute for the instructional services of live faculty.[2] Still, the centerpiece of nearly all varieties of asynchronous and synchronous formats is the lecture, supplemented by topical discussion groups, a resource library, and a detailed syllabus. In asynchronous environments, lectures take the form of text-based presentations posted to a Web site or audio/videotaped presentations that can be compressed and streamed over an Internet connection. In a synchronous virtual classroom, the lecture can be conducted through a PowerPoint presentation or a Web tour (that is, a class excursion to a Web site containing a lecture outline). Understandably, the lecture format provides students with the moorings of the traditional classroom in virtual space. Yet this confines the role of the teacher to that of being an information provider—reinforcing the minimalist definition of education that has facilitated its commoditization.

Technology and Creative Destruction

Educational institutions, like most corporations, have understood technology as a tool for organizational enhancement. Yet one of the striking lessons of the past few years is how established corporations have underestimated the impact of technological developments in their business environment. Technology is typically understood as a resource that enhances the status quo, not something that overturns it. This benign understanding presumes that the introduction of new technologies will allow organizations to be more effective or efficient at what they do.

Although it is undeniably true that technology often enables organizations to be better at what they have always done, in significant ways technology is a *disruptive* force that redefines the fundamentals of economic and organizational landscapes (see Downes and Mui, 1998, Kanter, 2001). The evidence suggests that technological change approximates Joseph Schumpeter's (1942) understanding of "creative destruction"—the process by which entrepreneurial innovation upsets the status quo and drives progress in a capitalist economy. Technologies of the "What hath God wrought!" variety—of which the Internet is a prime example—do more than open new promising vistas; they drop the curtain forever over significant portions of that which was.

The prevailing attitude toward distance education in the academy reflects a fundamental misunderstanding of the Gutenberg-scale invention that we call the Internet. As Carl Shapiro and Hal Varian argued in *Information Rules* (1999), the Internet has changed the fundamentals of the economics of information. Although information is still costly to produce, the Internet has revolutionized the way we *re*produce it, making it possible to reproduce information at a constant cost per unit that approaches zero. Furthermore, the number of copies that can be created and distributed on the Internet has no natural or physical constraint. This dramatically alters the concept of scarcity that underlies the whole of economic analysis. In this new economic environment, commoditization is something that should be avoided because price competition in a "frictionless" Internet marketplace will tend to drive costs down to roughly the additional amount it costs to produce an extra unit of information. This marginal cost of producing new information bundles will be very low—approaching zero.

If college and university administrators—along with entrepreneurial faculty members—expect a financial windfall from distance education offerings, they are in for a rude awakening, unless they have a plan to repeal the economics of the Internet. One professor enthuses that

> the Digital Age will resurrect the medieval model of the university, a model that puts teachers at the center of business, directly compensated for their performance. . . .
>
> As the Web becomes easier to use, and more professors get on-line, the public will become aware of the fact that education can occur without ivy-covered brick and mortar. As that happens, administrators will be disintermediated into oblivion, while faculty members will be elevated into independent, entrepreneurial thought leaders. . . .
>
> Your main concern will be figuring out how much to charge. . . . Aside from that, all you'll really have to do is prepare to teach and engage in some mild marketing—perhaps a few judiciously placed classified ads. [Glasser, 1999, p. B10]

A professor's livelihood does not currently depend on the market value of the information transactions that take place in the classroom. Students do not purchase specific parcels of information on the open market, but instead a package deal (a degree program) that gives them access to as much information as their teachers and campus library make available. Once the package deal has been purchased, these information transfers are perceived as being free—not counting the energy and effort needed to digest such information.

This model of free information transactions is being challenged in an interesting way with respect to faculty concerns over the ownership rights to course content and royalty arrangements.[3] The concerns surrounding faculty ownership rights, legitimate in themselves, appear to be based on the idea that lecture materials are so unique that they could compete in the open marketplace with other lectures on the same subject. This is clearly a faulty assumption. Given the remarkable uniformity of textbooks, why would one assume that on-line lecture content could profitably sustain its own market niche? For example, there is such similarity among major textbooks that a company named Final-exam.com is preparing generic study guides for freshman and sophomore college courses that students can access on-line—a kind of one-size fits all approach (McCollum, 2000a). Professors who envision a successful future in marketing their proprietary content on-line should ask themselves whether they consider their content to be the academic equivalent of the *St. Petersburg Times, Boston Globe, Washington Post, New York Times,* or *Wall Street Journal.* Other than the latter—the only on-line newspaper with paid subscribers—these newspapers' experience suggests that one would be lucky to break even, and more likely than not will end up losing money (see White, 2000).

Educators would be well advised to take to heart Esther Dyson's maxim to adopt the intellectual habit of treating proprietary on-line content *as if* it were free, focusing on ways to add value to it by offering related services (Shapiro and Varian, 1999). It appears that MIT has taken such advice to heart. In the spring of 2001, MIT embarked on a $100 million initiative to place its course content on the Internet, making it available free of charge (Carr, 2001b). While the idea of making course Web pages available to the public is nothing new, the scale of this initiative is striking. One is tempted to understand it as a mix of altruism and savvy marketing. As James O'Neill (2001, p. E3) notes, "In effect, MIT is saying: here, have all the course material you want. The material by itself holds little value. What makes a school like MIT worth the tuition is the value added to the raw information, through student-faculty interaction in classrooms and the learning opportunities available to members of an academic community."

The Trade-Off Between Richness and Reach

Philip Evans and Thomas Wurster (2000) of the Boston Consulting Group have developed a helpful analytical framework for understanding the dynamics of technology and creative destruction. In *Blown to Bits: How the New Economics of Information Transforms Strategy,* they argue that all businesses are subject to a trade-off between "richness" and "reach." Richness refers to the overall quality of information (for example, currency, accuracy, interactivity, relevance) and reach refers to the overall number of people involved in the exchange of information.

The significance of the new economics of information, courtesy of the Internet, is that it "blows up" the existing trade-off between richness and reach because information can be exchanged at the speed of light at virtually no cost. Even traditional brick-and-mortar enterprises, ranging from small retail stores to large industrial conglomerates, are affected by this change, as "information is the glue that cements vertical linkages together and defines a large portion of competitive advantage" (Evans and Wurster, 2000, p. 169). Consequently, entire industries face the prospect of being deconstructed because much higher levels of richness and reach can be achieved with the same bundle of economic resources.

Amazon.com is a classic example of how technology makes possible the simultaneous achievement of higher levels of both richness and reach in the bookselling industry. Amazon began as an idea in May 1994 as Jeffrey Bezos sat at his desk in the midtown Manhattan office of D. E. Shaw. He was surfing the Web and came across a site that announced that the Internet was growing at a rate of 2,300 percent a year. This got him thinking about the commercial potential of the Internet—which, at that time, was a commerce-free novelty. He started with a list of twenty products that could be sold over the Internet and narrowed that list down to two—books and music. He settled on books.

Bezos, then thirty years old, quit his job and headed West like the pioneers before him. The journey began on the weekend of July 4. While his wife, MacKenzie, drove their car to Seattle, Bezos drew up a business plan for Amazon on his laptop computer. Amazon.com was founded later that month. A little over five years later, Bezos was coronated as *Time*'s Person of the Year (Quittner, 1999).

Amazon.com's success is only partly related to its low prices and list of three million books—exceeding those of the largest chain store by a factor of twenty. It does not always offer the cheapest price, and Jeffrey Bezos did not create the database behind its book list—it had already been developed by industry wholesalers for the benefit of small bookstores. In its early days, Amazon.com ordered its books from two large wholesalers, unpacking and then repackaging them at its Seattle distribution facility. Amazon.com's success came about because it used technology and a strong commitment to customer service to improve the experience of buying a book (Polivka and Patterson, 1999).

As James Coates (1999) of the *Chicago Tribune* observes, Amazon.com offers most of the benefits of the megabookstores while restoring something of the personalized service of the small neighborhood bookstore. When a customer logs on to Amazon.com's site, he is greeted by name and informed of new books or CDs that are on sale or in the pipeline that seem like a good fit with his previous purchases. The availability of "purchase circles" makes it easy to browse titles of interest based on one's affiliations, and many people find the customer reviews of books to be helpful. "Does all this sound familiar?" asks Coates. "It should. It's the kind of stuff the folks used to chat about down at the neighborhood bookstore where everybody knew your name, until the giants ate them."

Evans and Wurster also cite the personal computer retailing business—a business focused on the sale and delivery of physical products—as a good example of the explosion of the richness-reach trade-off. If you navigate Dell Computer's Web site (www.dell.com), you can build a PC from a stunning array of options, using a configuration wizard that begins with your needs and the applications you plan to use. Dell implements this low-cost, customized approach to selling PCs with only an eight-day inventory of components and finished products! Think of how this compares with walking into a retail store and selecting a PC from a few models that have been sitting on the shelf for months. No wonder Dell is No. 1 in PC sales in the United States and worldwide.

In stark contrast to Amazon.com and Dell Computer, institutions of higher education have fixated on the "reach" side of the richness-reach trade-off. The distance education solution has been advanced as the means to accommodate the projected growth in student enrollments or extend the geographic reach of the marketplace for students. The fact that Internet technologies can simultaneously improve both the accessibility and the quality of educational experiences is rarely emphasized.[4] This pedagogical neglect of the richness side of the spectrum is all the more puzzling in light of the demonstrable richness that information technologies have brought to the tasks of research. One wonders whether this is just another manifestation of faculty priorities skewed in the direction of research over teaching.

The fixation of higher education on reach over richness does not bode well for the future. For example, colleges and universities are sitting ducks when it comes to their most lucrative source of tuition revenue—their undergraduate core curriculum. Fifty percent of the student enrollment at the community college level is concentrated in just twenty-five courses (introductory courses in English, mathematics, biology, psychology, chemistry, and so forth). At four-year baccalaureate institutions, these same twenty-five courses account for 35 percent of enrollment (Twigg, 1999). Most institutions long ago adopted a reach-friendly solution to these courses, consigning them to the impersonal environment of the large lecture hall. This approach had no justification in learning theory but was purely an economic decision.

Leaving aside its pedagogical shortcomings, the economic shortsightedness of delivering the core curriculum through the large lecture hall will likely become evident sooner than later. It will be relatively easy for commercial firms with substantial curriculum development budgets to develop on-line courses for the core curriculum that offer compelling richness at a lower price—perhaps working in collaboration with one or two academic institutions. Of course, one could always say that institutions of higher education will be able to defend themselves from such raiders of the core curriculum by their power to grant or deny transfer credit.

Realistically, though, the prerogative to grant or deny transfer credit is, at best, tenuous. First, institutions that join distance education consortia to market their courses—like the 262 institutions participating in the Southern Regional Education Board's Electronic Campus, which offers more than thirty-two hundred courses—will find it necessary to evolve seamless mechanisms for credit transfer. Once these mechanisms are in place (discussions for doing so are already under way at the Southern Regional Education Board), it will be politically untenable for colleges to bar transfer arrangements from commercial distance education providers, as long as the quality of the courses matches or exceeds those of the consortium. Second, internal pressure from students—who are always on the lookout for a good bargain—and the forces of market competition (that is, schools that offer more transfer credit will increase their competitive advantage) will virtually guarantee credit transferability and a hospitable environment for commercial firms.

The Broadband Virtual Classroom

Just as Amazon.com and Dell Computer have used technology to redraw the boundaries of the richness-reach trade-off in the sale of books and computers, the broadband virtual classroom holds similar promise for higher education—making it possible to achieve greater levels of richness and reach simultaneously. The integration of data, voice, and video into the "always on" environment of residential broadband will open up new possibilities for virtual learning. Students will be able to sit in front of a computer monitor and *participate* in a live lecture. They will not only be able to view PowerPoint slides while seeing and hearing the instructor but also be able to participate actively in shaping the content of the lecture. Unlike the passive environment of a large lecture classroom, the broadband virtual classroom will give instructors the opportunity to pepper lecture content with engaging questions that survey the opinion of the class—with the results immediately tabulated and displayed on the student's desktop. This facility could be used to great effect by a skillful lecturer. Instructors could also give students the opportunity to "vote" on how a lecture proceeds—for example, ask students which set of special topics or illustrations hold the greatest interest. Students would be able to have their questions answered on the spot by a panel of content experts (questions usually have a brief half-life of relevance). Raising one's hand in class and getting an immediate response is qualitatively different from waiting for an instructor's e-mail or logging on to a discussion board after a day or two. If a student has to miss a lecture, she could view a noninteractive version of the identical lecture at a later time.

Some may object that live lectures will crimp the style of students who want to take courses on an anywhere, anytime basis. However, when students compare the interactivity of the broadband virtual classroom with the loneliness of the self-paced, do-it-yourself course, they will likely embrace the minor inconvenience of sitting in front of their computers at a designated time. The typical high rate of noncompletion associated with standard distance education courses should give pause to those who need to be sold on the value of seeing and hearing a live teacher.[5] Moreover, students could be given a wide array of scheduling options to minimize the inconvenience of being in front of a computer screen at a particular time. Most important, the broadband virtual classroom will provide students with a reassuring educational experience that retains the look and feel of the traditional classroom while providing more interactivity.

The patent superiority of the broadband virtual classroom will leave the current narrowband post-a-lecture and host-a-discussion approaches to distance education in the dust. The broadband virtual classroom has more in common with traditional, classroom-based education than the prevailing narrowband approaches to distance education.

Distance education in its current incarnation has been accorded the status of second best. Tacit acknowledgment of this perception can be found in words of distance education advocates themselves. For example, one writer emphasizes the need for an appreciative audience as a critical success variable for distance learning (how many undergraduate instructors could count on this?). She writes: "Distance learning is especially useful for disenfranchised audiences, people who normally would not have the opportunity to take this course, but who would benefit from it. People who are forced to take a course will not be learners. That's why it's important to have an appreciative audience, people who want to take the course, who see some benefit from it, and who would not otherwise be able to take it at this time, for this cost, in a convenient location, and so forth" (Porter, 1997, p. 86). Even the tendency to emphasize convenience as an important drawing card of distance education reinforces its second-class status. The language of convenience often functions as a subtle cue to lower expectations for a particular experience. Something of some consequence must be given up for such anytime, anywhere flexibility; if not, we would have already witnessed the demise of the traditional classroom.

As odd as it may seem, the Home Depot may have more to do with influencing public perceptions about e-learning than educational institutions will. Why? Imagine the commercial potential of a broadband environment for a firm like Home Depot to develop first-rate courses with live instructors as a vehicle for building customer loyalty. Such courses could deal with a host of how-to topics, from remodeling a kitchen to seeding a lawn. A live instructor could contextualize a presentation to specific audiences and respond immediately to questions. Although it is unlikely we will be purchasing nails, lumber, doors, lawn mowers, and power-washers over the Internet anytime—although in Las Vegas, Nevada, the Home Depot is piloting a program to sell forty thousand do-it-yourself items on-line (Brooks, 2000)—some courses could feature prepackaged home kits that could be reserved on-line and picked up at the local store. Other courses might feature afterclass consultations with the instructor to put together a customized package of materials to be picked up later in the day.

Once the public actually experiences the educational potential of the broadband virtual classroom, it will only be a matter of time before parents ask why their son or daughter cannot use this technology to get a college degree, or busy single parents ask why they should wait any longer to go for their graduate degree. We may be a decade or more away from this moment, but when the benefits of the broadband virtual classroom become evident, change is likely to come quickly.

Mass-Produced Distance Education and Economies of Scale

How much would it cost to implement the broadband virtual classroom? Let us begin by picking an arbitrary tuition figure—say $100 per course, a figure recommended by William A. Draves, president of the Learning Resources Network ("A Distance-Learning Forecast," 1999). At that price, a course with a thousand students would generate $100,000 in revenue.

Let us give $20,000 of that to our lecturing professor as a gesture of appreciation. In the great academic tradition of undercompensating adjuncts, we are not going to be as generous with the content experts at the help desk. Assuming a ratio of one expert for every one hundred students, we will need ten content experts (perhaps placing another two or three on standby if our star lecturer has an obscure moment). If we pay each of them $2,000 per course, they could make a decent income working on twelve courses each term, or thirty-six hours per week—and they would cost only $20,000 for our course. We also need forty teaching assistants, using a ratio of one TA for every twenty-five students. Because that work could be done anytime, anywhere, it is likely that working professionals and some graduate students would agree to serve as TAs for as little as $1,000 per course to supplement their regular income.

We have $20,000 left over for incidentals and overhead. If we increased tuition slightly, to $125 per course, we could raise that contribution to overhead to $45,000.

Many personnel-intensive services could be rationed and subsidized on a fee-for-service basis. The same would hold true for access to on-line libraries containing books and academic journals. At a tuition rate of $100 to $125 per course, who would object to paying separate fees for student-teacher conferences, tutorial assistance, or a library book? Distance education providers could offer students a menu of support packages including a certain number of e-mail responses, teacher consultations, career counseling sessions, technical assistance calls, and the like. Such a system would be far more rational than the haphazard current model of unlimited access that allows some students to monopolize faculty time to the detriment of others.

The compelling economies of scale of the broadband virtual classroom will be the key economic factor that drives its development. It is telling that a recent study of the on-line MBA program at Maryland's University College, the for-profit subsidiary of the University of Maryland, found that a class size of fifteen students creates a loss of $22,399 whereas a class of twenty students yields a profit of $61,838 (Carr, 2001a). With the broadband virtual classroom, assuming a "correct" mix of support staff, class sizes could range from twenty to two thousand students, with no discernible difference from the student's perspective. Talented and well-compensated lecturers will be able to make effective use of humor, storytelling, and on-line polling to keep students' attention. Over time, with refinements in this instructional model, it would even be possible to reduce the number of content experts responsible for fielding questions during the lecture. Clarity is a desirable by-product of a polished presentation. Superficiality, a less desirable by-product, will also reduce the variable costs associated with keeping a staff of content experts on the payroll, although one should not assume that mass-produced distance education will be any more superficial than the surface learning of traditional classroom-based education.

Free College Degrees?

No one would balk at paying $100 or $125 per course, but there is every reason to believe that the price of tuition could eventually drop much lower. Perhaps it could even be free. Why? In a word, e-commerce.[6]

The concept of a free college education is, of course, hardly new. For over fifty years, Great Britain offered tuition-free postsecondary education until this policy was recently dropped (Reid, 1999). What is new is the idea that Internet technology makes it possible to deliver higher education programs for pennies on the dollar that compare favorably to the current fare offered by brick-and-mortar classrooms. This idea was brought to the national stage in March 2000 when Michael Saylor, chief executive officer of the software company MicroStrategy, announced that he was giving $100 million of his own money to develop a university that offers an on-line, Ivy League–quality education free of charge (Loose, 2000). Saylor's vision is based primarily on the use of streaming video technology. Students would receive lectures from world-renowned experts in their respective fields. With the fall of the NASDAQ in April 2000, the stock value of Saylor's company fell from a high of $333 in March 2000 to a low of $1.75 in April 2001. His vision of a free university has been reconceived as a "ten-year plan," and Saylor's pledge of $100 million will be realized by selling fifteen thousand shares of MicroStrategy stock each trading day over the next two years ("Software Magnate's Distance-Learning Venture," 2001).

Saylor's vision and generosity are indeed admirable. But there are good reasons to believe that e-commerce—not altruism—will deliver on the promise of tuition-free on-line education in ten to fifteen years. This model would also provide students with a much richer on-line educational experience than Saylor's streaming video approach.

Although it is very difficult to extrapolate long-term trends from the recent dot-com cycle of boom and bust, there are good reasons to adopt a rather rosy outlook on e-commerce. In this decade, the convergence of data, voice, and video over the Internet—coupled with residential broadband, wireless connectivity, and a host of Internet appliances—will give new meaning to the concept of being on-line. For good or for ill, the theological concept of omnipresence will have no better earthly exemplar than the Internet.

Some of the rethinking of the Internet that has taken place since the dot-com meltdown points to the fact that benefits of linking Internet technologies with the retail industry were more incremental than revolutionary. For example, the Internet component of consumer-based e-tailers is relatively small when compared to the brick-and-mortar logistics required to support these operations. Constructing a high-end Web site might cost between $15 and $25 million; a warehouse and distribution system, by contrast, can cost at least $150 million. These economic realities, coupled with the historically low price margins for the retail industry and the intense price competition made possible by the Internet, should have raised many red flags for investors and entrepreneurs who wanted a piece of the dot-com action. The fact that Internet technologies provide only incremental cost savings for retailing does not imply, of course, that e-commerce is dead. It simply means that this particular e-commerce application failed to deliver on unrealistic expectations (Mandel and Hof, 2001).

Educational services—unlike printed books, airplane flights, and electronic goods—can be delivered in a fully digital format. Consequently, there are some promising linkages between educational services and e-commerce. This fact has not been lost on on-line booksellers like Barnes and Noble. A company named notHarvard.com (now named Powered, Inc. at www.powered.com) has teamed up with Barnes&Noble.com to create Barnes and Noble University (www.barnesandnobleuniversity.com), offering a variety of free courses in the areas of arts and leisure, literary studies, life improvement, health and wellness, business, and technology (Carr, 2000c). The business case for Barnes and Noble University is that it will provide "stickiness" to its Web site. Stickiness is the measure of how long the average visitor spends at a Web site. Sticky Web sites encourage people to linger and "stick around," instead of casually hopping from one address to another.[7]

It would be difficult to conceive of a stickier venue than the broadband virtual classroom, where students could be captive audiences for forty-five to sixty minutes at a time. If e-commerce evolves into a fundamental fixture of the global economy, it is conceivable that a consortium of educational institutions and e-commerce companies could offer a low-cost, or perhaps free, college degree based on mass-produced distance education. Here is how it could work.

First, displaying advertisements on each student's computer desktop could generate a small portion of e-commerce revenues. The jury is out on the effectiveness of banner advertising on the Internet (Swisher, 2000; Streitfeld, 2000). Only about half of 1 percent of users click on the small banner ads that have become a ubiquitous fixture of the Internet. Larger ads have "click-rates" of 2 percent, and ads that involve animation (for example, elements fly out of the ad and around the screen) or tell a story with sound and motion have click rates from 7 to 10 percent (Hansell, 2001b). In the long run, though, it is not clear that more intrusive Internet advertising will be any more successful than the run-of-the-mill banner ads that most Internet users have easily learned to disregard. That said, one would imagine that advertising as modest as a corporate logo tastefully displayed in a virtual classroom could net thousands of dollars in revenue—particularly when such advertising dollars could be justified as part of the corporation's recruiting initiatives. For example, an investment banking firm could be the lead sponsor of a finance course, or a computer software firm could sponsor courses in computer programming.

Second, students could be asked to complete brief consumer preference surveys as part of the log-on routine for the course. This would be particularly attractive in light of advertisers' age preference and the demographics of a typical undergraduate classroom. One Internet site, FreeEdu.com, is already experimenting with this. It offers more than six hundred minicourses on a range of popular how-to subjects completely free of charge. The only catch is that students need to complete a marketing survey—what is called an interactive commercial—at intervals as frequent as every thirty minutes (Carr, 2000g).

The revenue potential of both of these approaches, though, pales in comparison to a third alternative: using the virtual classroom to establish shopping portals tailored to the interests of each student. This is where the real money may lie for e-commerce firms. The revenue model behind shopping portals is the concept of the *affiliate program*—an idea pioneered, and even patented, by Amazon.com ("Amazon.com Patent," 2000). Affiliate programs are revenue-sharing agreements through which commercial sites agree to share a percentage of their sales with the Web site that originally provided the link to the commercial site.

A study by Forrester Research found that 13 percent of the revenues from fifty Internet retailers in the United States came from affiliate programs. Each retailer had an average of ten thousand affiliates. Forrester predicts that by 2003 affiliate programs will account for 20 percent of on-line sales (Ellison, 2000). With

affiliate commissions usually ranging from 5 percent to 10 percent of the purchase price, it is not difficult to imagine the revenue potential of on-line educational programs that are packaged with shopping portals customized to the
student's interests. Some have speculated that the generous offers of Ford Motor
Company and Delta Air Lines to provide their employees with computers, print-
ers, and access to the Web for $5 to $12 a month were ultimately motivated by a
desire to create shopping portals. The companies' combined workforce of
422,000 represents billions of dollars in annualized buying power (Moozakis,
2000). However, since these programs were put in place, the interest in shopping
portals has declined and the benefits associated with having a wired workforce
are emphasized (Wagner, 2001).

It is reasonable to assume that even with expansion of e-commerce, potential revenue from advertising, interactive market surveys, or shopping portals
would not be enough to subsidize each student to the tune of $100 per course.
The era of giveaways and free services on the Internet is rapidly drawing to a
close (Hansell, 2001a). However, if a commercial subsidy covers just 50 percent
of those costs, reducing the tuition to $50 per course, this may be enough of a
subsidy virtually to guarantee free tuition in competitive market conditions. Why?
Once prices drop below $50, it is likely that at least one distance education
provider will seek to expand its market share by offering free tuition instead of
competing on the basis of prepackaged services (for example, career planning,
support groups) that are bundled with the virtual classroom. When one or two
additional firms follow suit, it will be difficult for the other firms to charge even
a modest tuition for broadband education unless a compelling case can be made
for the quality of their educational offerings. Even if e-commerce revenues
cannot sustain mass-produced distance education in the long run, firms will
dream up other ways to recover their costs. Most likely, zero-tuition pricing will
only be sustainable in the long term if these "free" educational offerings can be
bundled with other types of Internet services, such as premium digital media
packages (featuring "on demand" music and movies), that could be offered
through AOL and other Internet service providers (see Schiesel, 2001). If the line
between education and entertainment already seems blurred, it will grow more
fuzzy with the passage of time.

A significant side benefit of a low-cost or tuition-free college education is
that it would encourage the development of a personal service industry focused
on providing students with the motivational support to complete their courses
successfully—the academic equivalent of a personal fitness trainer. Such aux-
iliary support, which could take a number of innovative forms, would address
the significant problem of noncompletion in many current distance education
initiatives.

Making Peace with Commercialization

Certainly, many educators and some students will object to such blatant commercialization. Students could always be given the opportunity to pay the full price
for a course and avoid the distraction of advertisements, marketing surveys, or
shopping opportunities. It is a sure bet that most would opt for reduced tuition
over a commercial-free learning environment. Faculty concerns about placing lecture content in a parallel universe with commercial content could be allayed by
two lines of argument.

First, institutions of higher education are currently utterly dependent on the
social perception that a college degree has commercial value for those who own
it. If not for that social perception, it is likely that the demand would be limited
to intellectuals, artists, and those who seek some form of personal enrichment.
The demand for higher education that fills classrooms, expands course offerings,
and sustains research is built on a thoroughly commercial foundation. This is to
say nothing about the strong involvement of commercial interests in funding
research programs since the Bayh-Dole Act of 1980, which made it possible for
universities to secure patent rights to federally funded research (Press and Washburn, 2000).

Second, the juxtaposition of lecture content with the commercialization of
the virtual classroom could be made more palatable to instructors if they are re-
minded about multitasking behavior—that is, as discussed in Chapter One, the
ability to do several things at once. Put anyone in front of a computer screen,
ask that person to concentrate on a canned presentation, and before long he or
she will be viewing the presentation while having another window open to play
solitaire or check out a Web site.

Multitasking is irrepressible, and young people are especially good at it. John
Seely Brown (2000) relates the following incident: "Recently I was with a young
twenty-something who had actually wired a Web browser into his eyeglasses. As
he talked with me, he had his left hand in his pocket to cord in keystrokes to bring
up my Web page and read about me, all the while carrying on with his part of the
conversation! I was astonished that he could do all this in parallel and so un-
obtrusively" (p. 13). It is not unthinkable that a student could take in a lecture while
browsing through advertisements for the latest in video games, fashions, or automobiles. Unlike the traditional lecture hall, where students are forced to multitask
as a strategy for overcoming boredom, there is a strong likelihood that the engaging, multitasked environment of the broadband virtual classroom would increase the overall degree of student attentiveness to lecture content. Hence, a
behavior that is both unintended and undesirable from the standpoint of the

traditional classroom becomes an economic asset in the virtual classroom—perhaps even adding a little bit of value to the learning experience.

It should be emphasized that tuition-free college or graduate degrees could become a reality for some student populations without any *overt* e-commerce linkages.[8] Such programs could emerge from a corporate university model. For example, a university could contract with a large firm (or consortium of firms) to provide college and graduate degrees for its employees, perhaps initially specializing in identified skill and knowledge domains needed in that industry. At a tuition rate of $100 to $125 per course, this would be an irresistible bargain for most firms. Such online and customized educational offerings would be especially attractive if they were linked to companywide initiatives—like those of Ford Motor Company and Delta Air Lines—to provide employees with computers and Internet access (Brown and Swoboda, 2000; Thurston, 2000; Wagner, 2001). Furthermore, the increase in telecommuting—which will be given added impetus by the spread of high-speed Internet access—provides a ready-made infrastructure for the broadband virtual classroom. International Data Corporation projects that by 2003 roughly 13.5 million employees in the United States will work at home—excluding branch office workers and traveling employees (Wilde, 2000).

Government agencies will be similarly motivated to capture the benefits of e-learning. For example, the U.S. Army recently announced its plans to invest $500 million over the next five years in order to provide each soldier with a laptop computer, Internet access, and tuition for distance education courses (Carr, 2000a).

From a global standpoint, certainly the most compelling argument in favor of the linkage between e-commerce and mass-produced distance education can be found in the humanistic mission of higher education. It has been estimated that the creation of one university per week will be necessary if educational infrastructures are to keep up with world population growth (Daniel, 1996). This is a staggering figure. It is impossible to see how it could be feasible—on either economic or logistical grounds—to meet this global demand for education if not with e-learning.

Free, mass-produced distance education could fit the bill. Internet firms trying to open up markets for e-commerce in developing countries could largely absorb the costs of underwriting such global educational initiatives. From a marketing standpoint, it would be difficult to imagine a better way to launch e-commerce services to influential consumer segments. This raises important moral issues about the export of consumerism in the guise of higher education, but it is not inconceivable that the content of such curricula could emphasize the need for critical thinking about consumptive capitalism. A preeminent concern of any large-scale, global distance education provider would be to avoid charges related to cultural imperialism or the censorship of ideas.

The End of Education as We Know It?

If e-commerce and the broadband virtual classroom could bring about a golden age of free (or nearly free) education, perhaps even on a global scale, how will current educational institutions be able to compete?

The average annual rate of tuition among private four-year institutions in 2000 was $16,332, and loans increasingly prevail over grants in financial aid packages. Currently, 59 percent of all aid consists of borrowed money, compared with 41 percent in 1980 (Brownstein, 2000). The advantages associated with name recognition, a picturesque campus, and geographic proximity to the student's home will carry much less weight when the alternative is a free degree without the long-term burden of significant debt.

Clearly, the Internet is a two-edged sword. It opens up marvelous possibilities for a small college in Columbus, Ohio, to enroll students from Cairo, Cairns, Calgary, Caracas, and Cardiff. It also puts that school in a life-or-death competition with every other college, university, and consortium of educational providers on the face of the earth. Some schools may be able to profit from on-line offerings for a time but then experience steady erosion of their market position if they are unable to keep pace with the rapid decline of on-line tuition rates.

It is hard to argue with a free or nearly free education. Think of the anguish that most American households would be spared if they never had to ask the question, "How do we pay for college?" One should also keep in mind the highly misleading way in which educational services are currently priced.[9] Normally, a student cannot know the real rate of tuition until she goes through the process of applying to an institution of higher education and navigating the financial aid process. This is a much more time-consuming and stressful process than purchasing a home or buying a car, where the actual price of a good is reasonably clear after limited negotiations. Even the most complex commercial transactions, such as the sale or purchase of a business, are considerably more straightforward than the purchase of higher education. How many people have not realized their educational goals because of this arcane pricing system?

The commoditization of instruction assures that institutions of higher education that compete in the on-line marketplace will face tremendous competitive pressures. This process is already taking place in the market for retail products on the Internet. Comparative shopping services, like British Telecom's btspree.com service or DealPilot.com from Germany's Bertelsmann AG, provide Internet users with immediate price comparisons on a wide range of products (Pringle, 1999). It is only a matter of time before such comparative shopping sites dominate the distance education market, as they would not only publish helpful price comparisons but also student reviews of each course (similar to the customer review system currently in place on Amazon.com or eBay). Instead of running headlong into the beam of light emanating from the oncoming distance education caravan, administrators and faculty should have been thinking about differentiating their educational services by adopting strategies that add value to the educational experience and create a firewall against commoditization. By the time that many institutions recognize this strategic mistake, it may be too late to change course.

Strategic Options for Higher Education

The options vary depending on the institution's strategic assets and capabilities.

Top-Tier Institutions

Top-tier colleges and universities will likely emerge unscathed from the mass-produced distance education battle. Contrary to Peter Drucker's apocalyptic prediction that in thirty years "the big university campuses will be relics" and "the college won't survive as a residential institution" (Lenzner and Johnson, 1997, p. 127), I believe that the Ivy League institutions and their academic cousins will have the luxury of continuing with business as usual. This is not to suggest that top-tier institutions should be complacent in the face of a changing technological environment, but only that they can weather the changes ahead without great difficulty.

Although top-tier institutions will likely use their brand name to good advantage by offering e-learning programs of one type or other, these will not come cheap. They will likely be more expensive than their classroom-based educational offerings, and it is a sure bet that top-tier institutions will do nothing to threaten their prestigious standing in the marketplace. Two factors in particular virtually guarantee the continued prosperity of top-tier institutions: the exceptional downstream credentialing services of these institutions, and handsome institutional endowments—which have ballooned with the rising stock market during the 1990s—combined with a strong alumni donor base.

Ivy League institutions and their close cousins have excelled in providing graduates with robust credentialing services primarily because they have been able to invest their substantial institutional prestige in these services. Alumni are able to leverage this prestige in job interviews and informal contacts in a manner that yields great benefit in the labor market. The prestige factor drives firms with a healthy representation of Ivy League graduates to recruit "more people like us." The same dynamic works equally well in firms that boast fewer top-tier graduates in their ranks; the ability to recruit graduates from elite schools serves as a barometer of their up-and-coming status. In either case, resumes from top-tier schools rise to the top of the pile. Also, a credential from a top-tier institution best positions graduates for future educational upgrades if they decide to pursue them.

Because top-tier institutions have largely cornered the market on prestige, the interests of the institution, students, and alumni are strategically aligned in the direction of doing everything possible to enhance and maintain it. This explains why students (and parents) are largely indifferent to the reality that their high-priced education is often put into the hands of inexperienced graduate students or overburdened junior faculty, with limited classroom contact with senior faculty. At first blush, this makes no sense. But from a strategic standpoint, this arrangement is eminently reasonable because it provides senior faculty with the time and resources to continue to enhance the institution's prestige and social standing through their research.

Remarkably, it may be top-tier institutions, not the broadband virtual classroom, that will usher in an era of free undergraduate education. Tuition discounting and the aggressive competition for students means that on average, a $31,000 education is now sold for $8,400. It is not unthinkable that increased competition among top-tier institutions for the best students will not only produce effectively free tuition to such schools but even "negative tuition"—the best undergraduates will be paid stipends to attend. This conclusion seems radical until one realizes that top-tier Ph.D. programs have routinely paid students a stipend on top of free tuition for some time. The wealthiest institutions—those with substantial endowments and a strong alumni donor base—will be well positioned to attract the best students (Winston and Zimmerman, 2000). The existence of free, mass-produced distance education will have little or no impact on them.

Global Universities

A very small subset of the colleges and universities outside of the top tier will be able to take advantage of the demand for mass-produced distance education. These are likely to include a number of large universities and a few strongly entrepreneurial colleges—not counting a collection of yet-to-be-formed, for-profit virtual universities. These institutions have the opportunity to achieve the status of global universities through their distance education offerings—most likely working in close strategic partnership with at least one major textbook publisher or media firm and several e-commerce firms.

The global market for both higher education and continuing education is immense. The combination of pent-up demand for quality education and the development of strong global brands in higher education could stave off serious price competition for years. As a consequence, global universities will be in a position to make a great deal of money—particularly those based in North America and Europe, because of the increased status accorded to their degree programs throughout the developing world. It is not inconceivable that mass-produced distance education could be free (or nearly so) in developed countries because of aggressive price competition while remaining quite costly, at least for a time, in developing countries. One would hope, though, that such market imbalances would quickly disappear as new entrants to educational markets in the developing world began to satisfy the demand for education and price competition begins to take hold.

Somewhere between 75 and 150 major institutions could likely achieve this global university status over the next thirty years. In the long run, though, the number is likely to drop to the neighborhood of thirty to fifty schools because of the tremendous economies of scale associated with e-learning and the inevitability of aggressive price competition. Global universities would face few of the supply constraints that bedevil traditional businesses. The cost of adding one more student to a class roster of nine hundred or eleven hundred students is negligible, and there are no supply constraints to building as many classrooms as one would like, apart from those of bandwidth and server capacity. Both of these can be scaled up with relative ease. Furthermore, it will always be possible to secure the services of talented lecturers, skilled in the delivery of interactive lectures, through handsome compensation packages.

It is conceivable that the ranks of a single global university could swell to the millions. Although the very idea of such gigantic universities may seem ominous, the phenomenal scale of these learning organizations and their visibility in the marketplace will actually be beneficial in the evolution of educational standards across national borders. Furthermore, assuming the participation of big e-commerce players, these learning organizations may eventually compete for market share based not on the price of education but instead on qualitative factors. The only thing that might undercut the development of such desirable qualitative competition would be the practice of "bribing" students to take courses by means of some incentive payment. Such a trend seems unlikely now but is not impossible.[10]

All Other Institutions

Many educational institutions outside the top tier will be able to survive, and even thrive, in an era of mass-produced distance education if they can differentiate their educational offerings in an intentional, proactive manner. Depth education—the model of e-learning outlined in this book—is directed toward this group. Unlike the top-tier institutions, these colleges and universities will be forced to redefine their instructional services in a fundamentally new educational landscape. Although product differentiation could involve any number of innovative residential and off-site configurations, the twin features of cognitive apprenticeship and communities of inquiry will likely form the nucleus of these programs (the very characteristics that are absent from the broadband virtual classroom). In contrast to the largely impersonal character of mass-produced distance education, these programs will highlight the experiential dimension of education, providing students with learning experiences more substantial and durable than the information transaction approach of mass-produced distance education.

Education is a valuable long-term asset. People will not hesitate to invest their resources in education programs that open new horizons and empower them with transferable skills. Because of the greater amount of faculty-student interaction that occurs in depth education, smaller liberal arts colleges are likely to have a comparative advantage over larger universities in navigating this new educational landscape. Depth education also holds great potential for community colleges. These institutions have been among the early adopters of e-learning technologies, and the emphasis on cognitive apprenticeship through the use of knowledge rooms could enhance their status and respectability in the educational marketplace.

Institutions that fail to deepen their educational offerings will find themselves in a life-or-death competition. How do they compete with course tuition rates that look like the bill for dinner out for a family of four or that are even perhaps free? Unless they have something better to offer students, they cannot. Faculty unfortunate enough to lose their positions in the face of dwindling enrollments and dismantled programs would likely find work as content experts staffing a help desk for someone else's course—no doubt at a comparatively low rate of pay. This is hardly the sort of future one dreams of in graduate school.[11] A few unemployed faculty may even take positions as lecturers of on-line classrooms with seven hundred to two thousand students. Success in this arena will likely be handsomely compensated, but the simple joy of interacting with students may become an obscure memory.

The Saga of Britannica

Much of what was said in this chapter is, of course, speculative. No one can predict the future with any certainty. Yet those who surmise that the broadband virtual classroom poses no great threat to higher education should point their Web browsers to www.britannica.com and ask whether it would have been thinkable just five years ago to have the entire resources of the *Encyclopedia Britannica* at their fingertips—completely free of charge.

A few years ago, the thirty-two-volume hardback version of the encyclopedia cost $1,600 (it is still available for $1,250, with a few additional materials). Now anyone with Internet access is the owner of a fully searchable version of it, along with related articles from more than seventy magazines and links to over 125,000 Web sites. In a review of the site in *PC Magazine*, Don Willmott (2000) enthused that "it's probably worth the cost of a computer" (p. 150) to get access to such a valuable resource. He's right.

Of course, Britannica, a company in existence for over two hundred years with a brand name that is the envy of the Western world, is not giving away its content out of altruism but in order to survive. Beginning in 1992, when Microsoft entered the encyclopedia business with *Encarta*, the *Encyclopedia Britannica* has seen its position in the marketplace steadily decline. The company's first response was to offer libraries on-line access to the encyclopedia for $2,000 per year. Although large libraries purchased the on-line subscription, it was unaffordable for smaller libraries. Furthermore, the CD encyclopedias, like *Encarta*, which were being offered for less than $50, gained wide acceptance in the home market. By 1996, only four short years after the introduction of *Encarta*, Britannica's yearly sales of $325 million represented about 50 percent of what they were in 1990. Britannica responded to this decline by offering on-line access to home users in 1995 for a subscription of $120 per year and a CD version of the encyclopedia in 1996 for $200. After subsequent rounds of price-cutting to stimulate sales, both the on-line subscription and CD version failed to stem the company's need for revenue (Shapiro and Varian, 1999). By late 1999, Britannica had embraced the model employed by Netscape, Yahoo, and other Internet portals, giving away its content in exchange for advertising dollars (Rewick, 1999). By March 2001, in a bid for profitability, Britannica reversed course somewhat by reasserting a subscription model for an advertising-free version of its on-line encyclopedia. It also fired one-third of its workforce (Streitfeld and Cha, 2001). One can only hope that Britannica will be able to find some revenue model that will allow it to celebrate its three hundredth birthday in 2068.

The story of Britannica may reveal some of the changes that are likely to take place in higher education over the coming years. Accessible, mass-produced distance education is a great gift to the future that could transform the lives of millions, if not billions, of people. It will likely become one of the great stories of the twenty-first century. Yet the Britannica tale offers a cautionary note, as Evans and Wurster (2000, pp. 6–7) observe: "In dollar terms, sales of encyclopedias of all kinds are one-tenth of what they were in 1990. Microsoft never succeeded in getting to the price point it expected. Consumers rarely trade up from last year's promotional version to this year's fully priced version. Consumers benefit (if they ever use the product), but the industry is essentially destroyed. It is not clear that anybody will ever again write works of scholarship comparable to the greatest editions of *Britannica*—at least not in the same form."

Will liberal arts education go the way of the encyclopedia—a magnificent repository of knowledge and wisdom reduced to a cultural relic of the twenty-first century? If it does, the blame should be laid squarely on the shoulders of educators, administrators, and boards of directors. For too long we have underinvested in the classroom, and students have been socialized to expect less and less from education. The adventure of learning has been collapsed to what goes on the final exam. Getting the answer right counts for more than intellectual curiosity. More often than not, writing a "good" research paper means picking a topic that has been done to death. Intellectual risk-taking is only seldom rewarded.

We have the luxury of being able to look ahead and respond proactively. We cannot proceed on autopilot. The practice of teaching has not reached its pinnacle; much more remains to be done. Mass-produced distance education can only offer a shadow of in-depth and multidimensional learning experiences. Indeed, this may be a rare moment when the aims of educational reform are backed by economic necessity.

CHAPTER THREE

TRANSFORMING THE CLASSROOM INTO KNOWLEDGE ROOMS

Higher education remains captive to the working assumptions of an industrialized economy. Knowledge is acquired and certified in an assembly line process.

We begin with raw materials (students) and a set of production inputs (lectures and exams) organized in a standardized framework (course units). Production usually takes several years and processes the raw materials in a certain sequence (a degree plan with course prerequisites) that build toward a defined product (a diploma that certifies knowledge in a particular area). As with most assembly line processes, much energy is devoted to making sure that all individuals are doing their part to keep things going. The quality of the final product is secondary to the logistics of the process itself—each part must be assembled in the proper order.

Even our understanding of the course—the basic building block of the curriculum—is shaped by the assumptions of the industrial age. In the tradition of Frederick Taylor's scientific management, the curriculum is defined and controlled by experts. Accordingly, the course is built around their preferences and constraints rather than those of the learner. Furthermore, courses are usually organized around economic units of measure (credit units, seat time) instead of competency measures (performance outcomes), and participation in some courses is restricted to certain disciplines or depends on whether another course has already been completed (reflecting the industrial age penchant for hierarchical specialization). Finally, a common evaluation system is imposed on the course for the sake of standardization and comparability (Rowley, Lujan, and Dolence, 1998).

The lecture—itself an ancient and venerable academic institution—is the primary production input in the assembly line model. It is an exceptionally efficient means for parceling out information and has the added benefit of permitting the professor to put his disciplinary expertise on display, further legitimating the case for expert control over the curriculum. The professor defines his role by conveying information—telling students "how it is." Students are evaluated primarily on their ability to recall and restate what the professor said in class or what is contained in the textbook.

Linking lectures to exams bestows a kind of self-authenticating authority on the content of the lectures that it might not otherwise have. Even dated material that is recycled year after year takes on relevance to the final exam. Once students demonstrate a minimum proficiency in manipulating disciplinary methods and concepts in "textbook" situations, they are certified to proceed to the next course. Throughout this process, it is assumed that learning has taken place—despite an overwhelming body of evidence demonstrating that students quickly forget whatever they needed for the test.

As an institution in its own right, the lecture is so influential that even explicit attempts to discard it—by positioning teachers as classroom facilitators—fall prey to classroom dynamics that are perhaps even more unproductive. Not infrequently, the void that is created by removing the lecture is filled by a kind of stream-of-consciousness or free-form interaction that is almost confessional in character, lending an Oprah-esque quality to the classroom (Karabell, 1998; Perillo, 1997). Such discussion may have limited educational value, but instructors often consider them meaningful expressions of classroom participation, reasoning that at least they are not lecturing and the students appear to be somewhat engaged. It is almost as if the instructor's role is reactively defined more by what he or she does not do, instead of in terms of meaningful educational outcomes.

Higher Education and the New Economy

Although the assembly line model of higher education may have been a good fit with an industrial economy, it is strikingly out of place in an information-based economy. The skills required by the New Economy are not absorption and recall but discovery and discernment. Surface knowledge is of little value. Having the wisdom required to manage knowledge is quite another thing.

Because knowledge is a unique economic good, as there is no natural constraint on its growth, the basic problem for all knowledge-based economies is dealing with too much information—not too little (Shapiro and Varian, 1999). It is a wild guess, but some estimate that knowledge is currently doubling every five years—perhaps even less than that. This eclipses any other experience with exponential growth encountered by humans to date. If the human population increased at a similar rate, we would quickly run out of even standing-room-only space on the planet!

Information overload (or as one writer called it, *data smog*) is a common malady of our time (Shenk, 1997). The perception that the computer has not simplified but has instead complicated life is largely the result of this phenomenon. The more we know, the more anxious we become about what we do not know. Instead of preoccupying ourselves with questions of significance and having the wisdom to discern importance from detail, we are trapped in a Sisyphean cycle of trying to keep up with new information and perceiving that the more progress we make, the more we fall behind.

The focus of the input-output model of traditional education is on digesting preconfigured and sequenced bites of knowledge. This is not only out of step with the requirements of the twenty-first-century workplace but more importantly misrepresents what it means to be educated. Being educated is ultimately about being a better person—as in the ancient quest for wisdom and virtue. Education in the New Economy should provide students with opportunities for exploration and discovery in communities of inquiry as well as equip them with the skills they need to manage knowledge in an effective and ethical manner.

Recovering Communities of Learning

The commoditization of instruction has produced an academic culture that is preoccupied with the instrumentality of teaching services—whether a course will be taught by an adjunct or a full-time faculty member, whether it will be delivered in the classroom, by CD, or over the World Wide Web. Courses "materialize" when an instructor walks into a classroom or posts material to a Web site. Instruction becomes a production in which the teacher plays the roles of producer, director, and leading actor. This orientation has the effect of relegating students to the status of extras, obscuring the significant role they play in the creation of a vital learning environment. In academic contexts where the commoditization of instruction has not been allowed to flourish—such as the graduate programs of major research institutions—the integration of the student into a community of learning becomes a hallmark of the educational experience. This community of inquiry may consist of only one or two faculty members and a few research associates.

When students are deprived of such communities of learning, because of thoughtlessness or departmental dysfunction, graduate work becomes a great burden that leads to isolation and, often, despair.

One of the great benefits of e-learning—if it can be liberated from the depressing legacy of commoditization—is that it can help colleges and universities rediscover the value of communities of learning. It may seem ironic that technology would lead us back to one of the core building blocks of the humanistic mission of higher education, but in fact this should be no surprise. A yearning for community is what the Internet is all about. Mark Taylor, Webmaster for the City of Tucson in Arizona, summed it up nicely: "Two things made the Internet take off: e-mail and the ease of creating a Web page. It wasn't Disney's Web site. It wasn't Time Warner. It was the simple ability to send and receive messages; the ability to find a community of like-minded people by posting a Web page about your personal interests. These are the things that excited people about the Internet" ("Internet's Birth," 1999, p. 34).

In the Internet age, the computer is ultimately about connection. Kevin Kelly (1998), the founding editor of *Wired* magazine, makes this point when he declares: "Computers are over. Most of the consequences that we expect from computers as stand-alone machines have already happened. They have sped up our lives, and made managing words, numbers, and pixels quite extraordinary, but they have not had much more effect beyond that. The new economy is about *communication,* deep and wide" (p. 5).

The dramatic growth of the World Wide Web is a potent reminder of the human desire for community. In June 1993, there were 130 Web sites on the Internet (Gray, 1995). By June 2000, a mere seven years later, the Internet search engine Google (www.google.com) announced that it indexed more than one billion Web pages (Costello, 2000). Web sites and Usenet groups have wildly proliferated to cover every interest imaginable, including some that many of us would like not to imagine. Even computer video games—a socially isolating technology if there ever was one—have gained a distinctive social expression through the phenomenon of multiplayer Internet gaming. And contrary to all of the press that the Internet is breeding a culture of isolation, the Pew Internet and American Life Project (www.pewinternet.org) has found that the Internet actually enhances communication with friends and family members, particularly among women ("Pew Survey Disputes Notion," 2000).

The value placed on community in the Internet age is well grasped by observers of e-commerce (see Bressler and Grantham, 2000; Hagel and Armstrong, 1997). Customer loyalty and the degree to which people feel part of a larger community often go hand in hand. Amazon.com has been able to cement customer loyalty by encouraging its patrons to recommend books by posting reviews and to explore new titles by means of "purchase circles" (that is, groups of individuals with whom they have something in common) (Beck, 1999).

Perhaps the most striking illustration of the value of community in the world of e-commerce is eBay (www.ebay.com). Founded in the summer of 1995 by Pierre Omidyar, eBay began more as a hobby than an attempt to build an Internet business. The idea came to Omidyar when he heard his fiancée (now his wife)—who enjoyed collecting Pez dispensers—lament the difficulty of finding other Pez collectors to trade with in the San Francisco Bay Area. Recognizing the promise of the Internet for facilitating such transactions, he wrote some code over Labor Day weekend and launched AuctionWeb—a site accessed through the domain name of www.ebay.com. The eBay domain name stuck, and a new era of on-line auctions began, tapping into the American passion for flea markets and garage sales. In about five years, eBay has grown to include 22.5 million registered users and hosts more than 200 million auctions per year (Schwartz and Dobrzynski, 2001). In 1999, it had $4.5 billion in gross merchandise sales—a figure projected to grow to $15.5 billion by 2001. The company's net worth in 1999 ($20 billion) is more than the combined worth of Sears and J. C. Penney (Cohen, 1999)! eBay's most recent initiative is to allow sellers to establish virtual "storefronts" at the site for a modest fee (Wingfield, 2001).

As might be expected, the biggest problem for Internet auctions is giving people the confidence to bid on and purchase products from people they have never met before and with little more than a brief written description of the product, sometimes a picture. The solution for eBay was to create accountability by encouraging its customers to participate in a rating system that evaluated the reliability of both buyers and sellers. The rating system is voluntary and, of course, is not foolproof. But it has provided millions of people with the confidence to sell and purchase goods in conditions of relative anonymity. The rating system has been so successful that eBay now backs all of its transactions with a free $200 insurance policy. If a buyer purchases a product and never receives it or receives an item that is less than what was expected, eBay will reimburse him or her up to $200, less a $25 deductible. Assurances of this type, of course, would not have been possible without the phenomenal success of eBay's community-based rating system.

For many users, eBay has evolved into a meaningful space for community that features chat rooms organized by product categories, bulletin boards, space to create their own home pages, and a monthly newsletter. eBay volunteers form "neighborhood watch groups" to guard against abuse. Some "eBayers" have even been known to hold picnics and to take trips together or to help others out with home repairs. Beginning with the 1998 holiday season, eBay instituted a "Giving Board" where eBay members post requests for assistance to which others may respond (Kanter, 2001).

One of the more striking accounts of the sense of community among eBayers took place in early 1999. A woman who regularly participated in a discussion board about toy dolls suddenly disappeared. Other members of the "doll community" became quite concerned. They tracked her down and discovered that she had gone through a divorce. Her husband took the computer, and she was unable to purchase a new one. In response, several eBay members pooled their resources to purchase a computer for her (Bradley and Porter, 1999).

Certainly, community in an academic context should be even more valuable than in e-commerce. An academic community coheres because of its commitment to critical inquiry and respect for differences. There is also a strong ethic of service in vital academic communities, emphasizing the responsibilities associated with possessing knowledge.

The knowledge room model of depth education makes it possible to configure every course as an incubator for the development of robust communities of inquiry. One can also envision the development of more fruitful approaches to team teaching associated with the knowledge room model. With few exceptions, team teaching in the confines of a traditional classroom is a time-intensive venture with mixed results. Unless instructors develop a close working relationship, the benefits of a division of labor in teaching and grading responsibilities are outweighed by the logistics involved in planning a course and coordinating teaching roles. The knowledge room concept encourages educators to experiment with team teaching in the more restrictive sense of involving other educators as respondents in a seminar discussion or as guest evaluators for a research project. In addition, faculty would easily be able to incorporate the participation of selected alumni, or even colleagues at other schools, in order to enhance the depth and diversity of the learning experience.

The knowledge room concept also makes it possible to extend our understanding of academic community beyond the limits of matriculation and graduation by providing a platform for colleges and universities to offer a promising array of downstream and upstream services to their students (see Chapter Five).

A Work Group Paradigm for the Classroom

Depth education weaves together several important themes in the patchwork quilt of its knowledge room structure. These include cognitive apprenticeship, communities of inquiry, problem-based learning, knowledge management, embedded evaluation, and discovery-based learning. These themes are grounded in the core objectives of helping students to develop conditionalized knowledge and metacognitive skills. Toward this end, depth education uses what might be called a work group paradigm for the classroom.

The basic idea behind the work group model is to establish expectations in the classroom that rival those of the workplace, treating students like members of a virtual team. An individual does not advance in a career because she studiously takes notes or does well on exams but rather because she is able to work with people, communicate effectively, solve problems, explore opportunities, and assume leadership. The same should hold true for academic success. With the passage of time, workplaces of the twenty-first century will only become more challenging, not less so, requiring constant retooling and refining of skills. Why should the classroom fall behind in this game of expectations? If it does, we do a great disservice to students.

One primary benefit of the work group approach is that a teacher's time and talents are used more effectively. Neither lecture-based classroom education nor standard varieties of distance education make particularly good use of a teacher's gifts. There is only so much value added by repeating variations of the same lecture from one semester to the next or participating in on-line, stream-of-consciousness discussion strings. Bright and compassionate educators can be a lot more to their students than information providers or discussion facilitators. The work group model, in the context of cognitive apprenticeship and depth education, emphasizes the teacher's roles as model, coach, and most important, explorer.

Another exciting aspect of the work group or virtual team paradigm is that it could redefine the interface between students and key campus services—particularly library staff, writing specialists, and career planning staff. Resources in well-managed corporations are allocated in ways that increase the effectiveness of their work groups, and the same should be true of institutions of higher education. Normally discussions about technology and campus services focus on the mundane details of using on-line services to pay tuition, apply for financial aid, register for courses, or purchase books. Why stop there?

Why not, for example, prequalify writing assignments by taking a work flow approach to written assessment? Writing specialists could be directly involved in the assessment process for every student—not only when remedial attention is required. Much of the drudgery of teaching comes from the repetitive process of correcting papers. Although many educators take appropriate care in correcting spelling and grammatical errors on student papers, as well as engaging in some stylistic critique of their work, writing specialists can perform this important function in a more effective and consistent manner by using a work flow model. There is no reason why the evaluation of overall writing effectiveness cannot be separated from the evaluation of content. Such a division of labor makes great sense in light of the immense importance of developing strong writing skills—particularly during one's undergraduate career. Using inexpensive software programs like Markin32, a writing specialist could annotate a student's paper on the computer—having the benefit of a wide array of preprogrammed spelling and grammatical corrections and stylistic suggestions—before forwarding the paper to the professor for content evaluation (Carnevale, 2000b).

The work group model also opens up new opportunities for library and career planning staff to contribute directly to the classroom. For example, an instructor could include a career exploration component into a research project assigned for the course. The knowledge room framework makes it easy to incorporate members of the career services staff as resource navigators and respondents for such projects. Similarly, library staff can perform a tremendous educational role by serving as knowledge navigators for student research projects. Institutions would also be able to develop a rich array of specific tutorial services in the knowledge room framework of depth education, using collaborative tools like QuickPlace or Groove (www.groove.net) to host real-time meetings. It is worth noting that one company, SMARTHINKING (www.smarthinking.com), offers round-the-clock tutorial services for undergraduate students in core subject areas such as Spanish, U.S. history, and biology on a contract basis to colleges at the rate of $30 to $45 per student per semester (see Carr, 1999a). If schools can be assured of the overall quality and responsiveness of outsourced tutorial services, this will be a desirable alternative for many institutions.

Knowledge Rooms and Grassroots Change

A big strength of the knowledge room concept is that schools can adopt an e-learning framework and provide the necessary infrastructure improvements to support it without imposing a one-size-fits-all solution on educators. Faculty are free to incorporate as many or as few knowledge rooms in their courses as they choose. This is a great improvement over notoriously unsuccessful top-down approaches and the more common laissez-faire approach that A. W. Bates (2000) refers to as the Lone Ranger model.

The problems with top-down approaches to e-learning are legion. Chief among them is that they either don't work or wind up being isolated in one or two specialized programs that are marginalized from the mainstream of the institution. Top-down approaches also violate the collegial fabric and require a major up-front investment on the part of skeptical faculty with little promise of concrete returns. Because of the developmental complexity of most top-down initiatives and their inherent bias toward standardization, faculty are rarely able to implement e-learning projects without help from curriculum developers and technical personnel. The time required for them to interface with each new layer of specialists adds to the overall time commitment required of them.

The Lone Ranger model is less disastrous than the top-down approach but just as flawed. This approach tries to promote institutional change by a succession of pilot projects, using small grants and other support to encourage interested faculty to incorporate technology in their courses. The result is that many projects never produce a final product and those that do are often amateurish. The desire to empower entrepreneurial faculty is well intentioned but if at the end of the day one is left with an ad hoc collection of projects, it is unlikely that they will seed more substantive institutional change.

The value of the knowledge room concept and using a bottom-up teamware application like QuickPlace (most networking applications have a top-down bias) is that there are no intervening layers of technical specialists or curriculum designers between professors and their courses. This facilitates the development of an ethos of experimentation and a measured approach to technological integration—based on what really works to enhance learning, not the latest technology to come down the pike. The only institutionwide questions that need to be addressed are necessary infrastructure investments (discussed in the next chapter) and the development of a flexible formula for determining how classtime should be adjusted to reflect differing levels of knowledge room integration.

Constructing Knowledge Rooms

Knowledge rooms are built in two steps. First, you have to select the type of knowledge room you want to create. Second, you must assign a Web address for that knowledge room. Once a knowledge room is created, instructors or students do not need to be on-line to work in it. They have the option of working off-line, and changes are automatically updated when they can get access to the Internet.

Naming Conventions

It is strongly recommended that institutions establish guidelines for naming these Web sites in a uniform fashion. Using either course numbers with section names or the instructor's name as the primary component of the Web address, the address should specify the type of knowledge room being created and whether multiple versions of it will be used in the same course. The Web address should also specify the term and year in which the course is being taught.

For example, let us adopt the following abbreviations: R = Research Center, S = Skill Workplace, C = Conference Center, D = Debate Hall, P = Portfolio Gallery, M = Map Room, and A = Assessment Suite. Using these abbreviations, a Web site might be named as follows: the course number followed by a letter indicating the section (if any), the knowledge room designation, the term and year in which the course is being taught. For example, the second of five Research Centers for the fourth section of an introductory course in macroeconomics (Econ203) that is taught in the fall term of 2001 might get the following address: Econ203D-R2-F01. The address could also include the instructor's name instead of the section name or any additional specifications. The only restriction is that there can be no spaces, slashes, parentheses, punctuation marks, or accented characters in the Web address.

When instructors decide to construct a knowledge room, they are asked to select which type they would like to create (see Figure 3.1). Once they make a

FIGURE 3.1. SELECTING A KNOWLEDGE ROOM

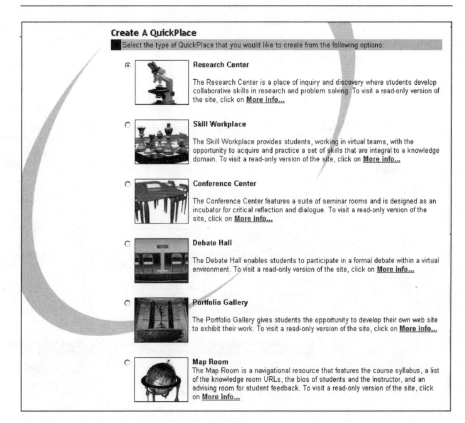

selection, they are presented with a screen (see Figure 3.2) that requests the Web address for the knowledge room. In addition, they are asked to provide their name, password, and e-mail address. When they have supplied this information, they may construct a preformatted knowledge room in less than a minute.

Adding Members

The next step is to add members to the knowledge room. Instructors can do this, or the task may be assigned to a teaching assistant. In addition, network administrators can use a tool called *placebots* to populate a knowledge room with members automatically.

When an instructor wants to provide students with access to a knowledge room, she simply clicks on the Members link that appears directly above the search tool for that knowledge room. When she clicks on the link, she will see that she alone is listed as a member of the site. By clicking on the Add/Remove Members link located in the upper left-hand corner of the screen, she is presented with the Add/Remove Members screen, shown in Figure 3.3. Other staff members (for example, writing specialists, research librarians, and career counselors) who may participate later in the course on a planned or ad hoc basis should be added to the knowledge room roster.

FIGURE 3.2 CONSTRUCTING A KNOWLEDGE ROOM

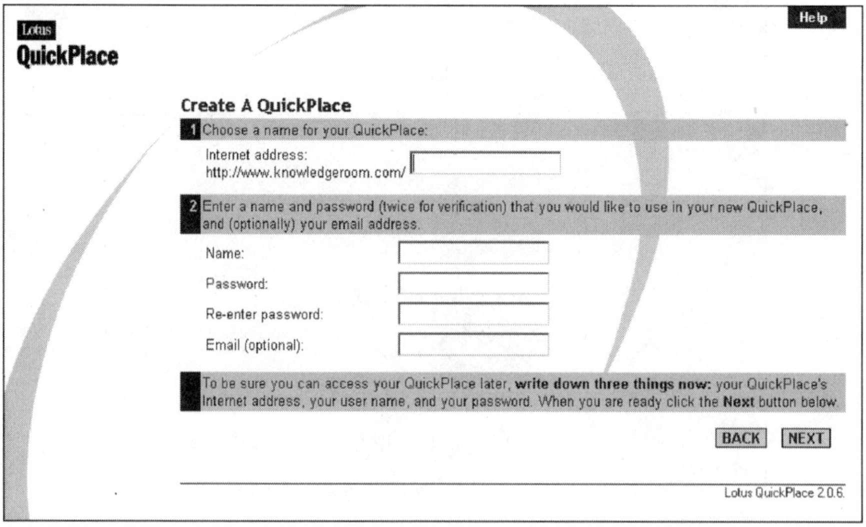

FIGURE 3.3. ADDING OR REMOVING MEMBERS

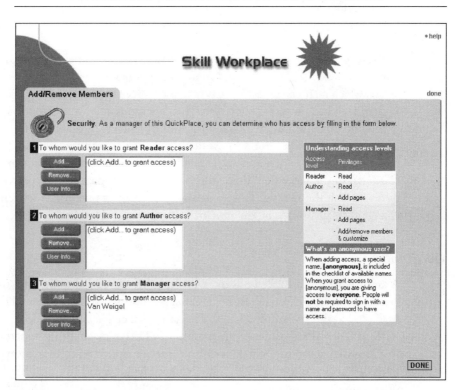

There are three levels of security available for each knowledge room: managers, authors, and readers. Individuals who have manager access can fully customize the site, add or remove members, create or delete inner rooms or folders, and perform other administrative functions. Those who have author access can add, delete, or edit any materials they have created on the site. Finally, those who have reader access can visit the knowledge room and examine its contents but cannot add or delete any material.

The creator of the site is automatically assigned manager access—the highest level of security. Managers can use a QuickPlace feature known as *themes* to experiment with different layouts for the knowledge room. They can also create inner rooms inside a knowledge room and limit access to each inner room to one or more students. Students do not need to remember any extra passwords to enter these secure inner rooms. They will only be able to see the rooms to which they have been granted access. For example, an Assessment Suite may house twenty assessment rooms, with each one assigned to an individual student. When the instructor logs on to a knowledge room, she will be able to see and access all twenty assessment rooms. But when students log on to the site, they will only be able to see and enter the one that has been assigned to them.

One of the typical problems associated with the assignment of user names in e-mail addresses and other applications is the limitation of eight or fewer characters, which restricts the use of first names or forces the truncation of last names. QuickPlace has no such restrictions. It is even possible to include spaces in a user name. For example, Van Weigel or Van B. Weigel are legitimate user names. This greatly simplifies the process of adding students to the knowledge room roster. In addition, when a member is added, an e-mail notification is automatically sent to the individual that contains the person's password and invites him or her to visit the site (this can be disabled for security purposes). Students may change their passwords at any time by clicking on the Members link.

PlaceTypes

A knowledge room is filled out by the content that is added to the site. Any Microsoft '97 or 2000 Word document, Excel spreadsheet, or PowerPoint file can be uploaded to the site automatically. The same is true for any graphics file with a .GIF, .JPG, or .JPEG extension. In addition, HTML files can be uploaded directly to a knowledge room. QuickPlace also comes equipped with its own text editor for creating new material for the site. No knowledge of HTML or other kinds of programming is required.

Much of this content will be added by students, but educators will want to prepackage a variety of informational resources with each knowledge room. Clearly, repopulating a knowledge room with these resources would be a very tedious task if educators had to start from scratch every time. Fortunately, a Quick-Place feature known as PlaceTypes makes it easy to transform any current knowledge room into a template for future knowledge rooms—reproducing the design and all the content contained in the original.

Two steps are required to create a PlaceType. First, the instructor (or whoever has manager access) selects the Customize link of the knowledge room and then clicks on the PlaceType Options link that is located under the heading Advanced Customization Features. From there, the instructor edits the PlaceType Options form, selecting which facets of the current knowledge room should be used as a template for future knowledge rooms. Once this is done, the network administrator can add that PlaceType to the list of options available to professors.

Sending Notifications

A powerful feature of QuickPlace is that it allows one to send e-mail notifications to members of a knowledge room whenever new material is added to the site through the Publish command. Such e-mail notifications can be automatically sent to all members of a knowledge room or to selected individuals. They can also be sent whenever a student or instructor visits a particular page on the site and would like someone else to look at that page. This is an especially helpful feature when directing guest evaluators (such as a faculty colleague or selected alumni) to certain sections of the site. Such announcements can be also used to great effect when an instructor wishes to highlight a particularly strong or inspired contribution to the site. All she has to do is navigate to the particular location of the knowledge room, click on the Notify link, and then add the e-mail address of the desired recipient. (By clicking on the word *To*, the student or instructor can select individuals from the knowledge room roster.)

Another helpful feature of QuickPlace is the ability to generate knowledge room newsletters—sent on a daily or a weekly basis—that keep everyone up to date on the additions that have taken place during the past twenty-four hours or the previous week. This newsletter is automatically compiled and sent by the QuickPlace server. The only involvement required by the instructor is to identify the kinds of updates that should be included in the newsletter. Once this is done, everything is performed automatically without further intervention.

These varied options for e-mail notifications perform the helpful function of reinforcing a sense of movement and dynamism. Both students and faculty are constructing something of value, something that invites the participation of others and deserves a special announcement. Although the value of such e-mail notifications can be cheapened with overuse, their judicious use can be motivational.

Holding a Meeting

QuickPlace contains a chat feature that is built into every knowledge room. When a student or instructor activates the chat feature, a separate browser window opens and he or she is presented with a list of the individuals who are present in the knowledge room *and* have activated their own chat consoles. If someone is working in the knowledge room but does not want to be bothered, that person is invisible when the chat console is closed. When others are in the room, messages can be sent to everyone or to specific individuals. Figure 3.4 illustrates one such conversation. Since it is reassuring to know that others are present in a knowledge room, the instructor should encourage students to activate the chat feature when they visit the room.

FIGURE 3.4. HOSTING A MEETING

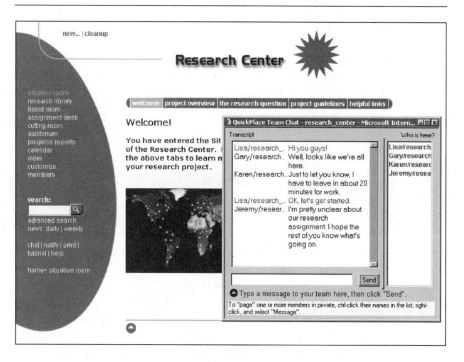

Knowledge Rooms and Cognitive Apprenticeship

We are now ready to explore the pedagogical aspects of each knowledge room. They are the Research Center, the Skill Workplace, the Conference Center, the Debate Hall, and the Portfolio Gallery. Table 3.1 presents a summary of the six methods of cognitive apprenticeship.

Table 3.2 provides an overview of the methods used in each of the knowledge room types. These primary knowledge rooms may be supplemented with two other rooms: the Map Room and the Assessment Suite.

Readers are encouraged to visit www.knowledgeroom.com and to construct one or two knowledge rooms on their own. There is also an on-line tutorial that accompanies each of the knowledge rooms.

TABLE 3.1. THE SIX METHODS OF COGNITIVE APPRENTICESHIP

Cognitive Apprenticeship Method	Description
Modeling	The teacher (or a student) puts her mind on display, walking students through the internal steps and strategies in problem solving, critical analysis, or creative development of alternatives.
Coaching	The teacher observes students in the performance of a task or skill (usually in the context of problem solving) and asks questions or offers feedback on their performance.
Scaffolding	Students are assisted by the teacher, their peers, or both in completing a task that they are unable to perform alone.
Articulating	Students practice the skill of converting tacit knowledge to explicit knowledge by describing the internal reasoning involved in problem solving or critical thinking exercises.
Reflecting	Students debrief and critique their own performance by comparing their approaches to problem solving and critical analysis with those of other students or the teacher.
Exploring	Students are encouraged to tackle new knowledge domains and problems on their own; the teacher stimulates intellectual curiosity and facilitates the discovery process (for example, guiding students in setting achievable goals or forming and testing hypotheses).

TABLE 3.2. KNOWLEDGE ROOMS AND COGNITIVE APPRENTICESHIP METHODS

Cognitive Apprenticeship Method	Research Center	Skill Workplace	Conference Center	Debate Hall	Portfolio Gallery
Modeling		√	√		
Coaching		√		√	√
Scaffolding	√	√	√		
Articulating	√	√	√	√	√
Reflecting	√	√	√	√	√
Exploring	√		√		√

The Research Center

The Research Center is the primary vehicle for the development of research and analysis skills. It also serves as an important incubator for leadership and communication skills. The Research Center features the following virtual spaces: the Situation Room, the Research Library, the Boardroom, the Assignment Desk, the Cutting Room, the Auditorium, Progress Reports, and Peer Review. There is also a group calendar built into the Research Center.

The Situation Room

When students enter the Research Center, they are ushered into the Situation Room (see Figure 3.5). This is where the research problem is stated and detailed. The folder tabs in the Situation Room feature an overview of the research project, a detailed description of the research question, a generic set of guidelines for the project, and links to Internet resources that are related to the topic.

FIGURE 3.5. THE SITUATION ROOM OF THE RESEARCH CENTER

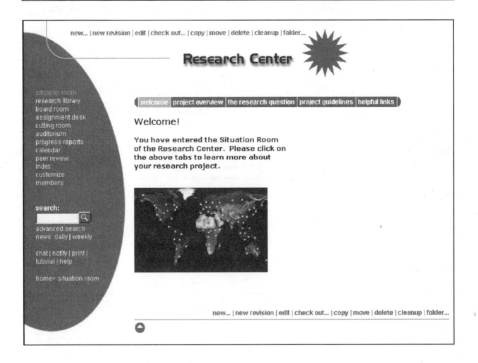

Project Overview. The project overview should provide students with an engaging orientation to the research project. The overview statement answers questions like "Why is research in this area important to advance our understanding of a discipline?" or "How might this research contribute to our understanding of human behavior or influence issues of public policy?" If the research project can be built around a case study or hypothetical scenario in order to create an ambiance of crisis, discovery, or intervention, this material can be incorporated into the overview statement or attached as a separate document.

The Research Question. The research question is a carefully worded statement that establishes the parameters of the research project. This statement may actually present several questions pertinent to the research problem. It should detail the main assumptions of the project and briefly outline what is not being studied.

Project Guidelines. Each Research Center should contain a generic set of guidelines that describe how research projects are evaluated and explain the responsibilities of each team member and those of the project director (leadership responsibility is assigned to one student for the duration of the project). It is also helpful to include a brief summary of the research tools available to each virtual team, such as on-line databases (which should also be referenced in the Helpful Links page), special collections in the campus library, area libraries available to students, and options for primary research (for example, surveys, interviews).

Helpful Links. This page should contain a list of Web sites, periodical databases, and search engines that students are likely to find useful in their research.

The Research Library

The Research Library serves as a document depository for resources collected by the students (all hard copy research materials should be referenced here). It may also contain prepackaged materials supplied by the instructor. Content that might otherwise have been included in course readings or lectures can be placed here, as long as it provides relevant background information for the research problem. In this way, an article, book excerpt, or lecture becomes more than just a required assignment; it becomes an information asset that is used to address a problem.

When the Research Library is already stocked with content, the first task of each research team is to create a knowledge digest of all the materials contained (or referenced). This is accomplished through a division of labor, under the supervision of the project director. All members of the research team are given the task of writing summaries of their assigned materials, emphasizing those points that are relevant to the research problem at hand. These summaries should be sufficiently detailed so that other members of the research group can review them and grasp the main points of each information asset.

Writing good summaries requires skills similar to those needed to take good notes—with one very important distinction. In preparing the knowledge digest, students must make their work intelligible and useful to others. This is a key knowledge management skill. Learning it also provides students with the opportunity to hone their skills in discernment (determining, for example, which parts of an article, lecture, or book except are relevant to the question at hand). In face of the growing problem of information overload, discernment becomes a particularly significant skill for the New Economy.

Because the members of the Research Center adopt a divide-and-conquer approach in preparing the knowledge digest, it is possible to prepackage a wide range of materials in the Research Library. This not only moves students beyond a homogenous textbook understanding of the issues but also makes possible the inclusion of both classical and cutting-edge contributions to the discipline—assuming their relevance to the research problem.

All members of the research team need to review the entire knowledge digest in order to help craft a research strategy for securing additional information assets. Therefore, when it is desirable for all members of the class to become familiar with the materials housed in the Research Library, instructors can assign identical copies of a Research Center to different research teams. This also helps students reflect on how their own research strategies and conclusions are different from those of other groups. Because members of the research team may only access their own Research Center until they release their findings, they will be able to conduct a true postmortem analysis of their own performance compared with other groups.

If it is not necessary for the entire class to be familiar with the prestocked contents of the Research Library, it is best to assign different Research Centers to each team as a way to lend breadth to the curriculum. Over time, once a full complement of Research Centers has been constructed, each with a different research problem, there is merit in allowing students to select one based on their own interests, thus forming research teams on a voluntary basis.

The Boardroom

The Boardroom is the brainstorming and problem-solving locus of the Research Center, serving as an incubator of sorts for creative and critical thinking. It is the place where team members debate alternative research strategies and reach consensus.

The Assignment Desk

The Assignment Desk features a project planning tool known as a Gantt chart. A Gantt chart is a visual management tool that depicts progress on different parallel and sequential tasks of a project in relation to a horizontal time line. It is the responsibility of the project director to assign tasks, hold team members to deadlines, and file a weekly progress report.

The initial responsibility of the project director is to oversee the preparation of the knowledge digest. His or her first task is to allocate the prepackaged contents of the Research Library to individual team members (accommodating personal preferences wherever possible). The project director is also responsible for coordinating the team's efforts to acquire new information assets (consistent with the overall research strategy). He or she must also appoint a managing editor for the research report and ensure that writing assignments are delivered in a timely fashion. Because students are given the opportunity to serve as project director on a rotating basis from one project to the next, the Research Center becomes a place where they can learn critical workplace skills such as leadership, communication, and time management.

The Cutting Room

Draft components of the research report are deposited, edited, and assembled in the Cutting Room, which functions as the editorial room for the research project. All members of the research team are responsible for drafting components of the research report and reviewing successive drafts of the report. For the sake of efficiency, the project director designates one team member as the managing editor. All the component documents put into the Cutting Room should be published so that all members of the research team can directly edit the document (this is done by clicking on the Publish As link in QuickPlace and using the Add Editors option). This approach helps students avoid having to reconcile changes in multiple versions of the same document. When one team member is reviewing and editing the document, he can check it out of the Cutting Room so that no one else will be able to edit the document at the same time.

As in the Research Library, discernment is a key skill learned in the Cutting Room—separating the important from the interesting and ensuring that the final document supports appropriate conclusions or enumerates questions for future research. There is also great value in the experience of preparing and editing a substantial report on a collaborative basis. Again, these are key skills for the twenty-first-century workplace.

The Auditorium

The Auditorium is the presentation room for the research project. The research report is presented here in a slide-show format that shows text (with or without graphics) in small parcels that are more readable than a single, long document. When the presentation is ready, the project director displays the site to the rest of the class by changing the security setting to allow for anonymous reader access (see Box 3.1). If several teams are working simultaneously on the same research problem, the instructor should have all the teams unveil their sites at a predetermined time.

BOX 3.1: CONFIGURING A RESEARCH CENTER FOR ANONYMOUS ACCESS

It requires just five clicks of the mouse for a person with manager access (for example, the student assigned to be the project director) to change the security settings of the site and enable anonymous reader access. When a knowledge room is configured for anonymous reader access, visitors to the site do not require a user name and password, but they also cannot make any changes to the site. This is considerably more efficient than going through the time-consuming process of adding user names and passwords so that the rest of the class can visit the site and offer their comments. It should be noted that when a site is configured for anonymous reader access, members of the research team must click on the Sign In link and then enter their user name and password to make changes to the site.

The steps for configuring a Research Center for anonymous reader access are as follows (manager access to the site is required):

- Click on the Members link.
- Click on the Add/Remove Members link.
- Press the Add button under Reader Access.
- Select the Anonymous checkbox at the top of the Add Readers form.
- Click on the Next button and then click on the Done button.

Progress Reports

The project director is responsible for completing weekly project reports that provide a snapshot overview of how the research is proceeding and identify problem areas that need the group's attention. These project reports are submitted with a special form that automatically publishes the report to the Progress Reports folder and sends an e-mail message to all members of the research team and the instructor, notifying them of the newly published report. Any of the team members, or the instructor, can comment on the progress report by navigating to the Project Reports folder and publishing a response. The form used to prepare progress reports provides the project director with the option of requesting a direct reply from the instructor.

Peer Review

All visitors to the Auditorium are responsible for reviewing the research report and offering their own critical assessment. Because each knowledge room is automatically assigned an e-mail address when it is set up, class members can e-mail their responses directly to the site. These assessments are gathered in the Peer Review area of the Research Center. Team members may access this area and discuss the reviews at their convenience. To make the Peer Review area accessible to all members of the research team, the project director (or anyone with manager access to the site) must enter the area, click on the Room Security link, press the Add button under Author Access, select the All Members checkbox, and then press the Next button. If an instructor wishes to make these evaluations accessible to the entire class after they have been submitted, this can be done by entering the Peer Review area, clicking on the Room Security link, pressing the Add button under Reader Access, selecting the Anonymous checkbox, and then pressing the Next button. It is recommended that instructors not make the peer evaluations public until all of the e-mailed evaluations have been submitted (to avoid any bias as a result of student evaluators reading the comments of other evaluators).

Each faculty member should prepare a set of guidelines for writing up a critical review of the presentation. Some professors may want students to offer their comments and suggestions to the research team without any reference to ranking or a graded assessment. Others may require students to rate specific aspects of the presentation on a four-point scale or assign a letter grade in addition to providing written comments. If an instructor decides to incorporate the Assessment Suite into a course, then students should also be required to complete one research team performance review for each research project. The forms for these reviews can be found in the Assessment Suite.

The Skill Workplace

The Skill Workplace is devoted to course content that requires knowledge mastery. The number of Skill Workplaces constructed for each course is completely up to the professor. Some may wish to consolidate all skill development in a single workplace. Others may wish to create several workplaces for the course that are built around key themes. Depending on the nature of the course, it may also be advantageous to incorporate several elective workplaces in a cafeteria plan structure, thereby giving students the opportunity to specialize in specific skill areas (for instance, the student could select two workplaces out of five or six).

In order to provide students with the satisfaction of completing one skill group before moving on to the next, it is best to avoid placing too many skill areas under one roof. This also enables the instructor to vary the composition of each virtual team from one workplace to another. The Skill Workplace consists of the following virtual spaces: the Lobby, the Office, the Exercise Rooms, the Help Desk, the Skill Gallery, and Team Reviews.

The Lobby

The Lobby is the entrance to the Skill Workplace (see Figure 3.6). Here students are introduced to the skills that they will acquire and practice in the workplace. These knowledge proficiencies may be confined to a few items or could cover a wide range of disciplinary concepts and methods. Using the folder tabs in the Lobby, the student can view a skill overview, the composition of virtual teams, a difficulty profile, a set of team guidelines, and an assessment statement that describes how individual and team performance will be evaluated.

The Skill Overview. The skill overview provides a general orientation to the skills that are covered in the workplace. This introduction should highlight the relevance of the skills for a student's continued work in a particular academic discipline or knowledge domain. Wherever possible, some mention of the practical relevance of these skills for different career paths is also helpful.

Virtual Teams. This page simply lists the names of students appointed to each virtual team and the Exercise Room to which they are assigned. It is best if each team consists of three students who are selected at random. The composition of the team remains the same throughout the life span of the particular Skill Workplace.

The Difficulty Profile. Not all skills are created equal. Based on the instructor's experience, this page alerts students to special difficulties they may encounter in learning one or more of the skills featured in the workplace. This difficulty profile may also present some learning strategies or simplifying concepts to help students overcome their anxieties about learning these skills.

Team Guidelines. Learning from one's colleagues is an integral skill of the New Economy. Accordingly, the Skill Workplace is built on the theme of peer collaboration. This page should emphasize the importance of team-based interaction for

FIGURE 3.6. THE LOBBY OF THE SKILL WORKPLACE

the mastery of skills. Because each team is responsible for working collaboratively on skill-based exercises and problems, instructors should include a generic statement that discusses the value of peer collaboration in the learning process and emphasizes the need for everyone to pull his or her weight. Instructors should also encourage those students who are more confident in their skills to field questions at the Help Desk.

Assessment. This page contains a brief statement explaining how work in the Skill Workplace will be assessed. It is recommended that instructors base their evaluations on the overall performance of the virtual team rather than try to distinguish each individual student's contribution to the group. The problem with this approach, of course, is that some students may rely on the efforts of more conscientious and energetic team members. This shortcoming, inherent in all forms of group collaboration, can be minimized by a system of peer accountability.

The Skill Workplace requires all students to complete at least one performance evaluation of their virtual team. The form for this evaluation, pictured in Figure 3.7,

FIGURE 3.7. THE TEAM PERFORMANCE REVIEW IN THE SKILL WORKPLACE

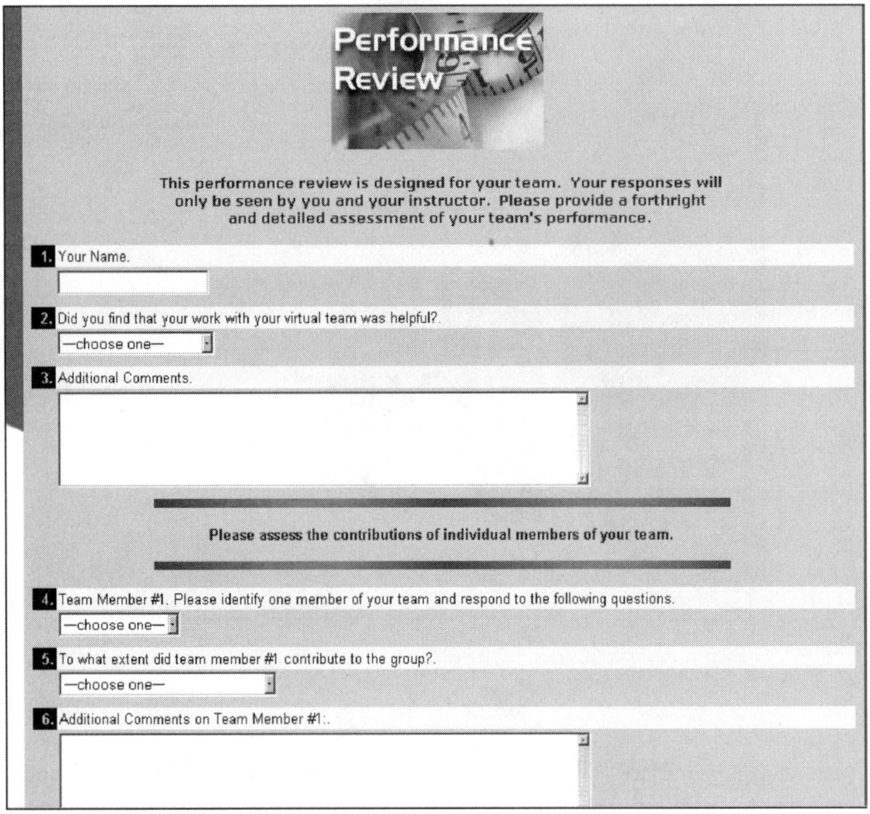
Performance Review

This performance review is designed for your team. Your responses will only be seen by you and your instructor. Please provide a forthright and detailed assessment of your team's performance.

1. Your Name.

2. Did you find that your work with your virtual team was helpful?.

—choose one—

3. Additional Comments.

Please assess the contributions of individual members of your team.

4. Team Member #1. Please identify one member of your team and respond to the following questions.

—choose one—

5. To what extent did team member #1 contribute to the group?.

—choose one—

6. Additional Comments on Team Member #1:.

can be modified by the instructor and accessed from any room in the workplace. When a student completes the performance review and publishes the form, the results are placed in the Team Reviews folder and the instructor is automatically notified by e-mail that it is there. Only the instructor and the student who filled out the form can view the performance review in that folder. This accountability system is further enhanced by the practice of mixing up the composition of virtual teams by using more than one Skill Workplace in a course. If a student shows a pattern of performing below expectations in two or more different virtual teams, this should trigger a discussion with the instructor at the very least, and most likely should figure into the student's final grade. Similarly, a consistent record of exceptional individual contributions to the group should also be reflected in a student's summative assessment.

The Office

All of the resources pertaining to skill development can be accessed through the Office. In QuickPlace parlance, the Office is an inner room, with its own set of folders and security settings—for all intents and purposes a Web site within the Web site. Unlike the Exercise Rooms, which are spaces assigned to each virtual team, all members of the Skill Workplace should be granted access to the Office (see Box 3.2).

BOX 3.2: THE SKILL WORKPLACE AND INNER ROOMS

The Skill Workplace makes extensive use of a QuickPlace feature known as *inner rooms*. The Office and Exercise Rooms in the Skill Workplace are constructed as inner rooms. Inner rooms are interior spaces (or Web sites within a Web site) that have their own security setting. Any single QuickPlace can accommodate an unlimited number of interior rooms; the only limitation is disk space on the server. The instructor (or a teaching assistant) can configure these inner rooms in the following manner.

First, all class members should be granted author access to the site. Clicking on the Members link and then selecting the Add/Remove Members link brings up the Add/Remove Members screen. Next, the instructor should press the Add button for author access, and the Add Authors page appears. The name, e-mail address, and password for each student are entered here, and an e-mail message is automatically sent that notifies the student of his or her user name and password. When the Next button is pressed, the Add/Remove Members screen reappears, and the Done button should be clicked.

Second, the instructor should navigate to the Office area and click on the Room Security link. This brings up the Office security form. Because the materials contained in the Office are only read or downloaded, they do not require anything more than reader access. Clicking on the Add button under Reader Access, selecting the All Members option, pressing the Next button, and then clicking the Done button accomplishes this.

Third, the instructor should navigate to each of the Exercise Rooms in the site and click on the Room Security link. This brings up the Exercise Room security form. Unlike the Office, the Exercise Rooms of the Skill Workplace require the active participation of students. Hence, they need to be given author access to these rooms. This is done by clicking on the Add button under Author Access, selecting the names of the students assigned to that Exercise Room, pressing the Next button, and then clicking the Done button. When students log onto the site, they will see only the Exercise Room assigned to their virtual team.

The Office and each of the Exercise Rooms have the same basic structure—they are all inner rooms and contain seven empty folders that are generically identified as Skill 1, Skill 2, and so forth. Therefore, the background information and learning resources stored in a particular skill folder housed in the Office has a companion set of word problems or case studies that can be found in the corresponding Exercise Room skill folder.

Most instructors will want to rename each skill folder to reflect the actual name of the skill. This can be done by navigating to the folder and clicking on the Folder link (for folder options). Because this is a tedious process (all of the changes in the Office must be reflected in each of the Exercise Rooms), faculty who use the Skill Workplace will want to develop a template that can be used as a model for constructing additional Skill Workplaces. This can be done through the PlaceType feature, discussed earlier, which makes it possible to use any knowledge room as a customized template for creating others. Therefore, all the materials that are prepackaged in the skill folders of either the Office or any of the Exercise Rooms can be reproduced in less than a minute.

The resources housed in the skill folders found in the Office could feature a wide range of materials (for example, text-based lectures, audio lectures, articles, concept papers, and book excerpts). With the increase in electronic books and customized digital textbook publishing (see Chapter Four), a lot of high-quality information could be incorporated into these skill folders on a selective, mix-and-match basis. Until that time, most instructors will find it necessary to use these skill folders primarily to reference assignments in external media associated with the course, such as printed textbooks or narrated PowerPoint presentations on CD-ROMs.

Exercise Rooms

Each virtual team is assigned its own Exercise Room (see again Box 3.2). The skill folders found in the Exercise Room contain word problems, decision scenarios, or case studies that correspond to the skill folders housed in the Office. It is the responsibility of each virtual team to divide the exercises equally (or nearly so) and begin to work on them individually. So there is no wasted time in figuring out how to distribute these exercises equitably, instructors should impose some type of folder-specific rule for allocating the questions randomly. For example, in one skill folder, the allocation of exercises could be governed by the alphabetical order of first names (so that Jan gets question 1, Michael has question 2, Patty has question 3, and Jan gets question 4, and so forth). In another skill folder, the allocation rule might be reverse alphabetical order or the alphabetical order of last names.

Team members are responsible to craft individual "solution narratives" in responding to their assigned exercises. A solution narrative not only presents the putative answer to the problem but also tells the story of how the student arrived at that answer. The basic idea is to track the cognitive steps taken in thinking through the problem, with the intended goal of developing the student's metacognitive skills. Obviously, such solution narratives only make sense when problems are interpretive and complex in nature. Once these solution narratives have been published to the site, it is the responsibility of another team member to publish a critical review of the narrative. With most word problems, this critical review may be no more than a brief thumbs up or thumbs down. For more interpretive decision scenarios and case studies—particularly those that require students to produce a document (for example, a corporate memo, a strategic assessment)—the critical reviews will be more involved.

As with the assignment of exercises for the solution narratives, a team member's responsibility to provide a critical review of another member's solution narrative should be assigned by a folder-specific allocation rule. For example, assuming a virtual team of three individuals, the educator could ask students to write reviews for solution narratives that directly follow or precede their own solution narratives, and then write a critical review for every third exercise. More complex allocation rules would ensure that the critical reviews received by any student were written by more than one team member (for example, having students use one allocation rule for 50 percent of the exercises and another for the other 50 percent).

This mix of solution narratives and critical reviews provides students with a rich canvas of problem-solving approaches for each skill under consideration. They also provide less confident students with a helpful scaffolding on which to construct their own solution narratives. Students not only benefit from viewing the solution narratives provided by other team members, discerning important commonalties in how their colleagues approach different problems, but also can seek direct assistance from the Help Desk (see the next section) if they "hit a wall" in working through a problem. The instructor's role is to offer guidance on a student's solution narratives (particularly word problems that have clear right and wrong answers) and to use the Skill Gallery to spotlight exceptional student work that can serve as a model for others. The instructor (or teaching assistant) is also responsible for managing the schedule of the skill workplace, using the QuickPlace calendar and notification facilities, to ensure that solution narratives and critical reviews are completed by the established deadlines.

The Help Desk

The Help Desk is the place where students can get assistance from more knowledgeable students in constructing their solution narratives. Moreover, students who provide the help have the benefit of mastering their own knowledge proficiencies by helping their colleagues understand a concept that may be obtuse or vague. The adage "You don't really understand something until you have taught it" has some truth to it. Practice in articulating concepts to others does deepen one's mastery of a skill. It is the instructor's role to review carefully such peer-to-peer interaction and to correct advice that is misleading or erroneous. As a last resort, the instructor should respond directly to a question if no one else is able to do so. With such close faculty oversight, student help providers can gain confidence in their own knowledge without fear of harming their colleagues with poor advice. They have the assurance that if they are wrong, the instructor will correct them.

Because of the significant educational payoff of the Help Desk to both help providers and recipients, it seems reasonable to reflect this service in a student's final grade. This may be done either by providing extra credit or factoring in exceptional performance as a help provider in computing the final grade (for instance, increasing the final grade by a half-step). There is, of course, a potential equity problem here, because students with a natural aptitude for the skill will be better positioned to serve as help providers. However, this problem is mitigated by the fact that help providers are contributing to the overall academic success of their student colleagues. Clearly, this plus-sum outcome benefits all students.

The Skill Gallery

One of the pronounced benefits of embedded evaluation, with its emphasis on developing the student's skills in articulation and reflection, is that a student's work can become a model for others. In this way, students themselves play an important modeling role in the classroom. The Skill Gallery is designed to capture this benefit for the rest of the class. Each virtual team can only see the outcomes of its own work, but the Skill Gallery allows instructors to draw on some of the best work of each virtual team, place it on display for all, and comment on it. With QuickPlace, this can be done easily with a few clicks of the mouse, by selecting the Copy link. In addition, the instructor may wish to send out an e-mail to notify all members of the class whenever the Skill Gallery is updated.

The Conference Center

The Conference Center hosts all the seminars for the course. Here students have the opportunity to unpack important themes in the course as well as explore and analyze new and controversial ideas—honing their skills in reflection, articulation, and critical thinking. Normally, a single Conference Center can accommodate an individual course because each one is divided into an array of topic-specific Seminar Rooms. Seminar Rooms can also be added on an ad hoc basis throughout the course. That said, some courses, particularly in the humanities, may feature several Conference Centers (just as more technical courses will have more Skill Workplaces). In addition, some instructors may wish to design assignments in which students create their own Conference Centers—hosting public forums that invite participation from outside constituencies (for example, coworkers, alumni participants, guest participants).[1] This has the added benefit of broadening the conversation and giving students the opportunity to convene seminars. The Conference Center features the following virtual places: the Lobby, the Reflection Pool, and the Seminar Rooms.

The Lobby

On entering the Conference Center, students find themselves in the Lobby (see Figure 3.8). Using the folder tabs in the Lobby, they can view the seminar topics and schedule, the seminar guidelines, a statement of how individual performance in seminars contributes to the final grade, and links to sample seminar discussions.

FIGURE 3.8. THE LOBBY OF THE CONFERENCE CENTER

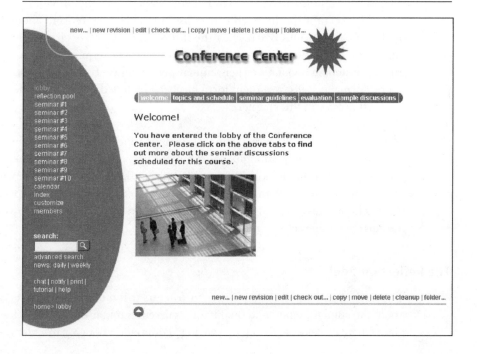

Topics and Schedule. This page lists all of the topics for the seminars and specifies the dates on which the seminars are active (generally no more than a week). It is a good idea to organize topics around appropriate themes. When a course makes extensive use of virtual seminars, perhaps scheduling two or three concurrent seminars, it is recommended that the instructor construct several Conference Centers, each designed around a particular theme.

Seminar Guidelines. This page should present generic guidelines for seminar interactions, such as respecting different opinions and valuing courtesy and collegiality. Students should be encouraged to offer their own critical appraisals of the opinions of other students, as long as they do it in a way that shows collegial respect.

Evaluation. Instructors are strongly encouraged to underscore the importance of thoughtful contributions to seminar discussions by considering the overall quality of the students' seminar interactions when deciding their final grade. By evaluating the quality of the students' contributions, educators can encourage them to take risks—giving special weight to contributions that are creative or make interesting connections to other knowledge domains. *The normal reservations about grading class participation in the brick-and-mortar classroom do not apply here.* Students do not need to vie with others to get a word in edgewise. E-learning provides the necessary reflection time for those who are constitutionally more reticent about weighing in on a discussion. Because of the inherently subjective character of such qualitative evaluations, instructors are encouraged to require a self-assessment from each student about his or her seminar performance. For this purpose, a seminar performance self-assessment form has been included in the Assessment Suite (see section later in this chapter).

Sample Discussions. Effective seminars do not happen by accident. They require high expectations for meaningful contributions from all participants. Therefore it is recommended that instructors provide links to three or four strong examples of previous seminars, so that students have a better idea of what is expected of them. These archived discussions, of course, should not include topics covered in the current Conference Center.

The Reflection Pool

The Reflection Pool is a place where instructors toss out their own observations about the content, tenor, and quality of a current seminar discussion. This is the place where professors can offer "weaving" comments about a particular seminar topic or theme. These are observations that bring together selected themes and contributions of a seminar discussion into a coherent framework. Students are also invited to make their own contributions to the Reflection Pool—either by responding to a professor's observation or initiating their own weaving comments.

Seminar Rooms

Each topic area should be assigned its own Seminar Room. Each Seminar Room should feature a controversial article, book excerpt, or case study placed on the table as a common point of reference for the discussion. This helps bring an analytical orientation to the discussion. When discussions do not have the benefit of such idea centerpieces, they tend to devolve into stream of consciousness exchanges and are of little use to anyone. In disciplines that are focused on the interpretation of texts, the professor may wish to place a passage from a classical work on the seminar table and request that students respond by offering their own interpretation or by parsing an important problem raised in the work.

Each student is required to publish his or her own thoughts on the idea centerpiece (using the New Page link). These responses may be understood as a sort of idea launchpad. Once the idea launchpads are published, students would be required to respond to at least three other idea launchpads or responses to them, based on their interests. Of course, there should not be any limit on the number of seminar responses. Popular idea launchpads could produce some very long threaded discussions. A student could also publish more than one idea launchpad, putting a different spin on the idea centerpiece and perhaps initiating a completely new discussion string.

One of the larger pedagogical payoffs of the Conference Center is that the classroom can be made more diverse by inviting alumni and other guest participants to weigh in on particular seminar discussions. People who agree to serve as guest respondents could be e-mailed weekly newsletters that notify them when a topic that matches their own interests and expertise becomes active. This brings a great wealth of experience and expertise to the classroom that would otherwise be unavailable.

There is also a promising intergenerational aspect to the Conference Center that may be exploited with great effect. Because each center—and the seminar discussions contained in it—can be archived for future use, it is possible over time to build a rich repertoire of discussion material that could be reviewed and critiqued by future generations of students. If the security setting of the archived Conference Center were changed to Anonymous Reader Access, then students would be able to review a previous seminar discussion, treating it as the idea centerpiece for the current seminar discussion.

Perhaps the most fruitful use of such intergenerational reviews would take the form of visiting a previous seminar that used the same idea centerpiece as the current seminar is using, reflecting on the different approaches taken by that earlier class compared with the current class. This could be easily accomplished by creating a link to the archived seminar, once the current seminar has run its course. In this way, students are exposed to a wider range of thinking and have a further opportunity to hone their skills in critical analysis.

The Debate Hall

The Debate Hall provides a virtual setting for formal debates. Like traditional live debates, these virtual debates are structured around a debate proposition and involve both initial presentations and rebuttals by the two opposing teams. The Debate Hall consists of four secure inner rooms that provide each team with preparation areas for both their initial presentation and their rebuttal. An additional secure space, labeled Debate Evaluations, collects the student evaluations that are e-mailed directly to the site.

These debates can be used to highlight dissenting methodological views in a discipline or to emphasize the relevance of a knowledge domain for public policy issues. In a virtual environment, students can present and assimilate more substantive arguments than would be possible during a live debate. A virtual debate also encourages thoughtful rebuttal statements. Most importantly, a virtual debate necessarily places the focus on the evaluation of content over style. Student evaluators and instructors alike are in a better position to evaluate the coherence of an argument and to assess the overall quality of the research marshaled in support of that argument. The Debate Hall includes virtual spaces for the following: orientation, initial presentation by the affirmative team, initial presentation by the negative team, affirmative rebuttal, negative rebuttal, and debate evaluations.

Orientation

Upon entering the Debate Hall, students are provided with an orientation to the debate (see Figure 3.9). Using the folder tabs, students can view the debate proposition, the debate schedule, the members of the affirmative team, and the members of the negative team.

Debate Proposition. This page contains the debate proposition and provides some context for why the issue is relevant for the course. If the debate involves a methodological rift in a discipline, then some historical storytelling can be done to provide students with a disciplinary context for the debate.

FIGURE 3.9. THE DEBATE HALL

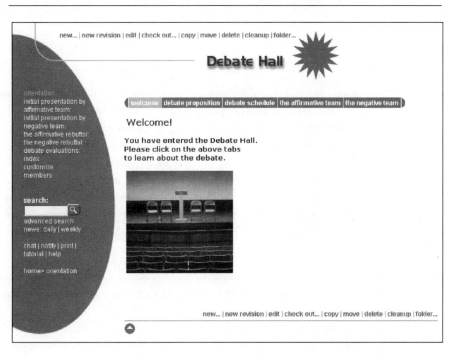

Debate Schedule. Although the Debate Hall has an asynchronous format, allowing students to access the debates anytime and anywhere, this does not mean that time is inconsequential in sequencing each stage of the debate. The instructor must impose specific deadlines in scheduling the debate. The first deadline is the due date for the initial presentation of the two opposing teams (the affirmative and negative presentations are unveiled simultaneously). The second deadline is the completion of the rebuttals by both teams. Like the initial presentations, both the affirmative and the negative rebuttals should be unveiled at the same time. Finally, there should be a due date for the submission of all debate evaluations, which are then made public after this deadline has passed.

Affirmative and Negative Teams. These pages list the names of the students participating in the debate. The students' pictures may also be included, along with some brief details of their respective backgrounds and what interested them in the topic. In the spirit of friendly competition, instructors may want each team to introduce itself, perhaps making use of humorous self-portraits or fabricated biographical statements that boast of their qualifications for this debate. If the teams are given this option, they must be added as editors to these pages. Clicking on the Edit link and then pressing the Publish As link will bring up the Add Editors option.

Affirmative and Negative Initial Presentations

The primary stage of the debate is the development of the initial presentation by the two teams. Each team has its own secure area to prepare this presentation, complete with a resource depository for research materials, a boardroom for crafting a strategy for the debate, a cutting room for editing the presentation, an assignment desk to coordinate tasks, and a team calendar. These collaborative spaces parallel those of the Research Center. Box 3.3 explains how these designated areas can be configured by the instructor or teaching assistant. At a designated time, these initial presentations are simultaneously displayed to the opposing team, and the debate enters its rebuttal phase.

BOX 3.3: CONFIGURING THE DEBATE HALL

The first step is to grant author access to all members of the debate team. Clicking on the Members link and then selecting the Add/Remove Members link brings up the Add/Remove Members screen. Next, the instructor should press the Add button for author access, and the Add Authors page appears. The name, e-mail address, and password for each member of the affirmative and negative teams are entered here, and an e-mail message is automatically sent to each debate participant, notifying him or her of the user name and password. When the Next button is pressed, the Add/Remove Members screen reappears.

The next step is to configure the entire site for anonymous reader access. This is done by clicking on the Add button under Reader Access and then checking Anonymous, located at the top of the Add Readers screen. When anonymous reader access is granted, it means that visitors can access the site without a user name and password, but they cannot make any changes to the site. When members of the debate team access the site, they must click on the Sign In link and enter their user name and password. This will allow them to access their designated debate preparation areas.

Following this, the instructor should navigate to each debate preparation area (for example, Initial Presentation by the Affirmative Team) and click on the Room Security link. The instructor will see his or her name listed under Manager Access. Because each team should have full control over its respective debate preparation areas, team members should be granted manager access to that area

---

BOX 3.3: CONFIGURING THE DEBATE HALL, continued

only. Clicking on the Add button under Manager Access, selecting the names of either the affirmative or the negative team, and clicking on the Next button accomplishes this.

Finally, when both teams have completed their initial presentation, as stipulated in the debate schedule, the instructor (or each debate team) unveils the initial presentation by clicking on the Room Security link. This is done by pressing the Add button under Reader Access, selecting the Anonymous option, and clicking on the Next button.

This last step is also repeated when the affirmative and negative rebuttals are completed and ready to be displayed.

Affirmative and Negative Rebuttals

The rebuttal phase of the debate should normally be completed within forty-eight hours after each team has released its initial presentation. Both the affirmative and the negative teams have their own secure spaces to prepare their rebuttals, including a Rebuttal Notebook that can be used to assemble and organize talking points that can be used in responding to the initial presentation of the opposing side. When the rebuttal statements are completed, they are released at a predetermined time and the evaluation phase of the debate begins.

Debate Evaluations

Up to this point, only the instructor and four students have accessed the debate site. Now that the formal phase of the debate has concluded, the remaining students in the class are invited to visit the Debate Hall and submit their debate evaluations. As in the Research Center, these student evaluations can be e-mailed directly to the site—because each knowledge room is automatically assigned an e-mail address when it is set up—and they are automatically collected in the debate evaluations area. In these evaluations, students should cite the strengths and weaknesses of the initial presentations and rebuttals. They should also indicate which team they believe won the debate. When the deadline for the evaluation phase of the debate arrives, the instructor should make these evaluations accessible to the entire class by entering the Debate Evaluations area, clicking on the Room Security link, pressing the Add button under reader access, selecting the Anonymous checkbox, and then pressing the Next button and clicking on the Done button.

The Portfolio Gallery

The Portfolio Gallery is the simplest knowledge room to configure. It is also probably the most powerful. Here students have an opportunity to place their work on display and benefit from the feedback of their student colleagues. In effect, the student, working alone or with another student, designs his or her own Web site around a particular theme or project. Unlike a research paper that is submitted in a single draft, read by the instructor, and returned to the student with a summative assessment, the Portfolio Gallery is built on the model of peer review and refinement. When a portfolio project is ready to be placed on display, visitors to the site can e-mail their own critical reviews and constructive suggestions. These reviews, read by the creator or creators of the project portfolio and the instructor, are used to improve the site. Consequently, the Portfolio Gallery highlights the profoundly social context of research and emphasizes student accountability to a community of inquiry.

Each Portfolio Gallery includes a project planner and a group calendar, accessed through the Tasks and Calendar links. These resources are particularly helpful if more than one student is working on the portfolio. The Portfolio Gallery consists of the following virtual places: the Rotunda, the Gallery, and Reviews.

The Rotunda

On entering the Portfolio Gallery, students are in the Rotunda (see Figure 3.10). Using the folder tabs in the Rotunda, they can access a brief orientation to Quick-Place that explains how to create folders, add pages, and add links to other sites, and how other students can submit their reviews of the site. There is also an on-line tutorial available to students. These instructions would be deleted when students construct their own Web sites.

Creating Folders. This page explains how to create folders. Folders are a way of organizing content in a readable and inviting format. Students may create as many folders as they wish. Moreover, if they choose to reorganize their content in the latter stages of a project, this can be done easily in QuickPlace because folders may be deleted and reconfigured without deleting their content. New folders can be given content by going to the Index, clicking on the Cleanup link, selecting the appropriate documents, and copying those documents from the Index to a particular folder. Most students will use either the headline format (used in the Rotunda folder) or the slide-show format (used in the Gallery folder) in organiz-

FIGURE 3.10. THE ROTUNDA OF THE PORTFOLIO GALLERY

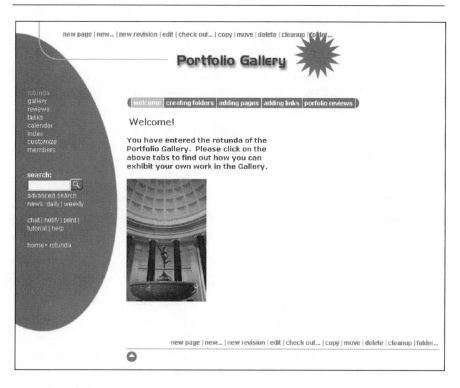

ing their portfolios. It is also possible to create folders that accommodate threaded discussions or folders that allow visitors to rearrange a long list of documents in a different order.

Adding Pages. This section briefly explains how pages can be added to the Portfolio Gallery. To add new content, students may either click on the New Page or New link. The New link allows them to import existing documents or to create new documents from Microsoft Office, create new folders, and add pages that link directly with another Web site. File attachments can be added to site by clicking on New Page and dragging and dropping files from a desktop into the attachment area. New content is uploaded to the site by clicking on either the Publish or Publish As links. When two students are working on the same project, one of them can directly edit pages added by the other by clicking on the Publish As link in QuickPlace and using the Add Editors option.

Adding Links. This page warns students that, because of copyright law, they should take great care not to reproduce content from other Web sites. However, when they find content that is relevant to a presentation, they can develop links to those sites and should be encouraged to do so. They can do three things to link to another site. First, they can add a link to any page by clicking on the Insert Link button, located on the far right of the toolbar on the QuickPlace text editor (accessed by clicking on New Page). Second, they can create a link by clicking on the New button and selecting Link Page from the list of options (to minimize confusion, link pages should always be opened in a separate browser window). Third, they can simply type in the Web address in the QuickPlace text editor, and it will automatically create a link (for example, www.britannica.com).

Portfolio Reviews. This page briefly explains how visitors to the Portfolio Gallery can submit e-mailed reviews of the site (see the section below on reviews).

The Gallery

The Gallery folder is based on the slide-show format. This folder type features Next and Back buttons that allow a visitor to view an exhibit in sequential order. Because project portfolios should make generous use of folders, most students will want to incorporate several gallery folders—each organized around a particular theme or component of the portfolio. Students should also experiment with the use of the headline folders, which feature page tabs at the top of the screen (these folders are limited to no more than five to seven pages, depending on the length of the page title).

Students should be encouraged to be creative in designing the site. They should also be made aware of how white space and an uncluttered presentation can improve the look. They should make liberal use of tables (using Microsoft Word or Excel), and graphics should be incorporated selectively (that is, graphics should not be used for their own sake but only to illustrate content effectively).

Reviews

When it is time to unveil the site to the rest of the class, students should click on the Members link. From there, they should click on the Add/Remove Members link. This brings up the Add/Remove Members page. By clicking on Add button under Reader Access and clicking on the Anonymous checkbox, anyone can visit the site without a user name or password (they will also not be able to alter the site in any way). Other members of the class can now view the site without a user name and password (and the creator of the site must click on the Sign In link to make changes to the site).

Critical reviews and constructive suggestions can be directly e-mailed to the site. The e-mail address is based on the name of the portfolio, followed by the @ symbol and the domain name of the site (for example, my_portfolio@ knowledgeroom.com). These e-mailed reviews are deposited in the Reviews section of the site. It is strongly recommended that these reviews only be accessible to the creator or creators of the portfolio project and the instructor. In this way, student evaluators will not be biased by reviews already deposited at the site. More important, this is consistent with one of the principles of embedded evaluation: *public* peer-to-peer evaluations should be restricted to peer-to-team evaluations; individual work should not be evaluated in public (see Chapter One).

To allow instructors to read and respond to these student reviews, the portfolio owner must first grant the instructor author access to the site by clicking on the Members link and then selecting the Add/Remove Members link. This brings up the Add/Remove Members screen. Next, the portfolio owner should press the Add button for author access, and the Add Authors page appears. The name, e-mail address, and password for the instructor should be entered here, and an e-mail message is automatically sent to the instructor, notifying him or her of the user name and password. When the Next button is pressed, the Add/Remove Members screen reappears and the Done button should be clicked. After that, the portfolio creator should enter the Reviews section and click on the link for Room Security. Next, using the Add button under Author Access, the instructor's name should be checked so that he or she can read and respond to the student reviews. If significant changes to the site are required as a result of this feedback, it is recommended that the portfolio owner temporarily remove the anonymous reader access setting to make these changes.

The Map Room

The Map Room is a supplemental room that serves as a navigational resource for students (see Figure 3.11). It houses the performance outcomes for the course, the list of assignment and projects, the course schedule, and the criteria used to evaluate student performance and to assign course grades. The Map Room also consolidates all of the URLs for the course in a single page. In addition to these navigational aids, it contains separate folders for brief biographical statements from the instructor and each of the students. In order to facilitate the rotation of the project director role in the Research Center, it is recommended that students

FIGURE 3.11. THE MAP ROOM

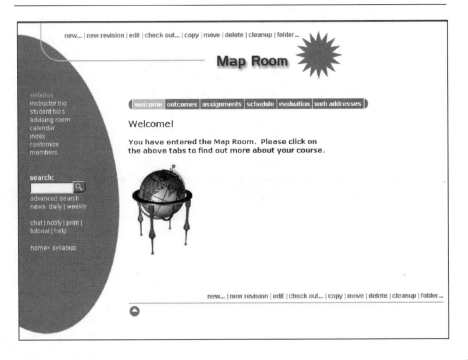

list the last three times that they have served as a project director (indicating the date of service) on their bios. The Map Room also features an Advising Room that is designed for rapid student responses about the course. Here students can advise faculty of issues and problems and make constructive recommendations for improvement.

The Assessment Suite

The Assessment Suite houses a set of secure inner rooms, assigned to individual students, for performance reviews and grade reports (see Figure 3.12). The Assessment Suite presents the criteria for evaluating student performance and determining course grades (these are identical to the evaluation statement featured in the Map Room), along with the institution's guidelines for the grade appeal process. It features self-evaluation forms for students to assess their overall performance in the Conference Center, the Debate Hall, and the Portfolio Gallery.

FIGURE 3.12. THE ASSESSMENT SUITE

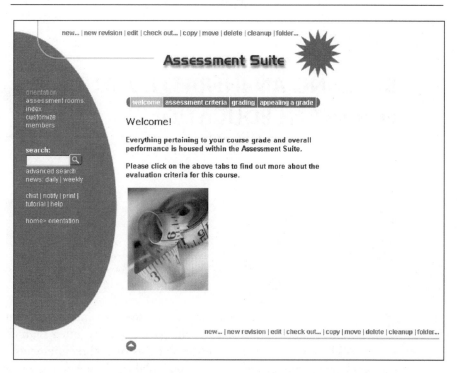

These self-evaluation forms can be accessed by clicking on the New link. Students may also access a research team performance review form here. It is far superior to use assessment rooms for evaluations than to deliver them to students by e-mail or include them as marginal comments on a paper. This approach not only sees evaluation as an opportunity to establish a dialogue between professor and student but also creates a permanent record of all interactions in a secure space.

We are now ready to explore the infrastructure of the knowledge room learning architecture.

CHAPTER FOUR

BUILDING AN INFRASTRUCTURE
FOR DEPTH EDUCATION

Depth education does not require smart classrooms, wireless campus networks, or significant technical skills on the part of faculty (other than the ability to use a Web browser). The make-or-break infrastructure requirements for depth education are more conceptual in nature, and they begin with faculty.

The Infrastructure Begins with Faculty

Five faculty development initiatives are particularly important: confronting the crowding-out effect, offering formative evaluation, working with virtual teams, developing weaving skills, and understanding copyright law.

Confronting the Crowding-Out Effect

What I refer to as the *crowding-out effect* is the lack of clear knowledge priorities in the curriculum. Unless these priorities are established, the sheer volume of course content will continue to crowd out meaningful opportunities for students to learn. In order to master a skill, practice is essential. Superficial exposure contributes little to a student's knowledge base. Think, for example, about how you first learned to use a computer.[1] Did you sit down and carefully read through a manual before turning on the computer? Did you take a course and complete a battery of exams? Or did you turn on the power switch and set out to learn one or two applications, such as a word processing program or a Web browser, by trial and error? You probably took the latter course. And when you ran into a problem, you consulted a manual, or more likely, a knowledgeable friend, to resolve it.

One factor behind the curricular crowding-out effect is the legacy of behavioral psychology. Behaviorism proceeds from the assumption that the learner is passive and requires some form of external motivation and reinforcement for learning to take place (Skinner, 1953). The task of education, from a behaviorist perspective, is largely to provide students with a road map for the acquisition of information and skills. Each information parcel and component skill becomes a milepost along the road, sequenced in a hierarchy from simple to complex. The main challenge, from a pedagogical standpoint, is to keep students moving down the road. Sustaining such motivation requires a mix of positive and negative incentives. Consequently, "educators spend their time developing a sequenced, well-structured curriculum and determining how they will assess, motivate, reinforce, and evaluate the learner. The learner is simply tested to see where he or she falls on the curriculum continuum and then expected to progress in a continuous, quantitative fashion as long as clear communication and appropriate reinforcement are provided. Progress by learners is assessed by measuring observable outcomes—behaviors on predetermined tasks" (Fosnot, 1996, p. 9).

Professors who are especially gifted communicators or adept at creating user-friendly tests get extra points for playing the role of information salesperson or appraiser. Students are major "beneficiaries" of the system because it is relatively simple to determine which mileposts must be taken seriously and which can be safely ignored, thereby hastening their educational journey.

The influence of behavioral psychology is particularly evident in what might be termed the *miniaturization of skills*. The bias of behaviorism is toward bite-size chunks in skill acquisition. A skill is assumed to be cumulative in character, so that small skills can be compiled (often at some undisclosed later date) into larger and more useful ones. The miniaturization of skills is further aided by the naming convention of treating applied concepts as skills. It works like this. Take a concept and apply that concept to a set of preformatted (or textbook) problems. Voilà! A skill is born! If one assembled each of these component skills at the conclusion of the course, students would be left with little more than a composite of all the concepts introduced in the course—not a set of skills that were practiced and refined in different contexts. The general discomfort experienced by countless students—as expressed in such phrases as "I really don't know what I really learned in this course"—is not entirely attributable to the sentiment expressed in the old adage "You know more than you think you do." It is the consequence of their dealing with a patchwork quilt of bite-size skills—proficiencies rarely mastered to any degree or integrated in a larger, coherent framework.

Establishing clear knowledge priorities is a key responsibility of educators. Some blocks of knowledge are essential for a discipline, others are desirable for the sake of comprehensiveness, and still others may be considered elective. Typically teachers make these distinctions informally by knowing which chapters in a textbook to skip or deemphasizing some lecture topics to place more emphasis on others. But depth education requires a more intentional approach.

One way to prioritize course content is to rethink the curriculum in terms of the core integrative skill of knowledge management. This approach begins with the question, "What do I need to know to manage knowledge in this discipline?" Although the response obviously depends on the discipline, some generic answers are easily identified. First, students must learn the concepts and specialized vocabulary of the discipline. Second, students need to have a working proficiency in the methods used by the discipline to gather, organize, and analyze information, as well as to solve problems and generate new disciplinary knowledge. Third, they need to understand the significant historical advances made by the discipline— not only to gain an appreciation for the importance of this knowledge domain but also to reinforce the idea that all knowledge is a work in progress. Fourth, they need to be familiar with the leading edge contributions of the discipline; these provide some understanding of the likely future trajectory of the discipline and its relevance for other knowledge domains.

The knowledge management matrix (see Exhibit 4.1) is a helpful way to differentiate the skills that are integral to a discipline from those that may be preferred but are not necessary. It requires the prioritization of four knowledge types into three categories. The knowledge types are concepts (including specialized vocabulary), methods (including specific techniques), historical contributions of the discipline or field, and leading-edge contributions of the discipline or field. The three categories are knowledge mastery, knowledge familiarity, and knowledge elective. Because of the disciplinary focus of the knowledge management matrix, a single matrix may be constructed for several courses. But the matrix can just as easily be applied to a single course, assuming that each knowledge type applies to the particular disciplinary slice covered by the course and not that of the entire discipline.

The primary dilemma for educators is to draw the line between knowledge mastery and knowledge familiarity in a discipline's concepts and methods. It is not easy to do this. Faculty must set aside their syllabi and textbooks and ask themselves some hard questions about the kinds of knowledge proficiencies (concepts and methods) that are necessary, making the required adjustments for under-

EXHIBIT 4.1. THE KNOWLEDGE MANAGEMENT MATRIX			
Knowledge Types	Knowledge Mastery	Knowledge Familiarity	Knowledge Elective
Concepts			
Methods			
Historical Contributions			
Leading-Edge Contributions			

graduate and graduate environments. Thankfully, most skills that relate to a discipline's historical contributions and nearly all of the leading-edge contributions will fall into either the familiar or the elective categories. This simplifies somewhat the task of constructing a knowledge management matrix.

In the knowledge room framework of depth education, skills that require knowledge mastery should be incorporated into one or more of the Skill Workplaces. Mastery requires practice, and practice is not sufficient if it is restricted to one or two contexts (because the student does not have the opportunity to abstract the performance of the skill from the details of its application). The four other knowledge rooms—the Research Center, the Conference Center, the Debate Hall, and the Portfolio Gallery—can accommodate those skills that require knowledge familiarity or are considered knowledge electives.

Offering Formative Evaluation

In the embedded evaluation approach of depth education, educators try to seek a balance between formative and summative evaluation. Because they have considerably more experience with the summative types of evaluation that are associated with grading exams and papers, it is helpful to provide faculty with development experiences in which they explore the value and methods of formative evaluation. One of the points to emphasize is that formative evaluation should never become a straightjacket for summative evaluations. Educators often find themselves in a double bind when it comes to formative evaluation. An instructor offers suggestions for improvement, the student complies with these suggestions, the instructor gives the assignment a grade of B, and the student contests the grade on the basis that he did everything the instructor requested. Suggested improvements may be a road map for improving one's grade, but they are not an implicit contract for an "A."

Working with Virtual Teams

Because three of the knowledge rooms—the Research Center, the Skill Workplace, and the Debate Hall—are structured around the concept of virtual teams, faculty development experiences on the cultivation and nurturing of virtual teams would be very helpful. A key characteristic of well-functioning virtual teams is that all members are clear on their individual responsibilities (Lipnack and Stamps, 1997; Harasim, Hiltz, Teles, and Turnoff, 1995). In the Research Center, it is the job of the project director to assign research tasks, submit progress reports, and hold team members accountable. In the Skill Workplace and the Debate Hall, the instructor assumes some of these managerial tasks by default (although they could easily be delegated to teaching assistants).

The team performance review in the Skill Workplace and the self-evaluation forms found in the Assessment Suite are designed to help students evaluate the overall value of their virtual team interactions and assess the quality of their own individual contributions. Some of this reflection could also be done by e-mail response to four or five questions about process posed by the professor. Here are some possible questions (Palloff and Pratt, 1999, p. 128): (1) How well did I participate in my group? Was I a team player? (2) Did I make a significant contribution? (3) Did I share my portion of the workload? (4) How comfortable do I feel with the group process? (5) Did I feel comfortable expressing any problems or concerns openly? (6) Did I provide substantial feedback to other group members? (7) How do I feel about the collaborative work produced by my group? (8) How well did the collaborative process contribute to my learning goals and objectives for this course?

It is also a good use of regular on-site class time to give students the opportunity to air some of their questions and concerns about virtual teams.

Developing Weaving Skills

A skill necessary for educators in all varieties of e-learning is weaving student contributions into coherent observations or conclusions. The weaving process not only helps students integrate course material and see the big picture but also emphasizes their important role as knowledge creators. In performing this function, faculty demonstrate that they are listening to students and reflecting on their ideas with collegial respect. Therefore, a good weaving message will refer to specific ideas that students have contributed instead of to generalities (Harasim, Hiltz, Teles, and Turnoff, 1995). Being specific allows educators to select especially strong contributions and build on them. This reinforces the value of communities of inquiry to the work of education and can have a long-term impact on a student's self-confidence.

Teachers should never underestimate the effect of seemingly insignificant gestures of professorial respect for a student's ideas. Take, for example, the following reflection from Dale Marshall, the president of Wheaton College in Massachusetts and the former dean of Wellesley College:

> I still remember vividly how lonely I felt when I walked into my dorm room at Cornell University for the first time. . . . Two conversations with experienced Cornellians also helped tremendously in making me feel at home. The first was with a professor in an introductory political science class. Knowing that it is hard to adjust to new academic expectations, he took special care after the first mid-term to talk about writing essay exams. Then he read portions of student answers as examples of how to write good answers. Mine was one of the anonymous examples used. That gave me courage to talk with him after class, and the ensuing friendly informal conversation ended my reticence about talking to professors (and probably started me on the path to becoming a political science professor myself). [Pillemer, Picariello, Law, and Reichman, 1996, p. 319]

There is no higher compliment that a professor can give his or her students than to acknowledge publicly the value of their work.

Understanding Copyright Law

One of the thorniest issues facing e-learning is the digital use of copyrighted material. The furor over the sale of dissertations and journal articles on Contentville.com—a venture launched by Steven Brill, founder of *Brill's Content,* in collaboration with CBS, NBC, and others—underscores the ambiguous character of copyright issues in the Internet age (Blumenstyk, 2000b; Rose, 2000). Current copyright law has failed to keep pace with the digital revolution. Furthermore, infractions of copyright law are so pervasive on the Internet that common practice ceases to be a good indicator of whether copyright infringements are taking place.

The fundamental copyright challenge in a digital environment is finding ways to control access to intellectual property so that it is difficult or useless to duplicate and distribute protected materials. When you purchase a CD or videotape, you are buying access to intellectual property—not the rights to reproduce and distribute it. The same holds true for digital music files. The problem is that digital material can be duplicated and distributed to millions with little effort and cost—unlike taping a favorite CD and giving it to a friend. Once such intellectual property is released in a networked environment, the owners of it are no longer in control of their legitimate rights to reproduce and distribute it.

It will not be easy to find solutions to this problem, but technologies related to digital rights management (or DRM) offer some promise (Weber, 2000a). DRM technologies focus on sealing content in a tamper-proof protective wrapper that can be accessed only by persons who have the correct "cyberkeys" or placing content in digital lockers that can be accessed without the need to make a local copy. Electronic books may hold the key for a lasting DRM solution in academic contexts (see Weber, 2000b). Obviously, the ultimate fate of DRM technologies will depend entirely on whether they are accepted by consumers.

For e-learning, the most problematic aspect of current copyright law is the definition of the fair use of protected materials—for instructional purposes—in an electronic environment. There are three problems with current fair use guidelines: they are only guidelines that reduce the risk of suit but do not fully protect institutions from copyright infringement suits; they call for limitations that make no sense in an educational context (for example, music educators can only use 10 percent of a recording or thirty seconds, whichever is less) (Willdorf, 2000); and they allow the use of audiovisual materials, such as movies, for instructional purposes in a face-to-face classroom but not in an on-line environment. This last issue concerns the so-called classroom exemption stated in section 110(1) of the 1976 Copyright Act.

The Digital Millennium Copyright Act—signed into law in 1998—took note of this problem and required a study and report to Congress on whether and how copyright law should be modified to facilitate distance education. This study, entitled *Report on Copyright and Digital Distance Education*, was delivered to Congress in May 1999. The recommendations offered were very favorable to the instructional use of copyrighted materials in distance education. Educational institutions would also have the responsibility to take measures to protect those materials against unauthorized access, provide protection against the unauthorized dissemination of those works after access was acquired, use only lawfully acquired copies of copyrighted works, and educate the campus community about copyright restrictions (Gasaway, 1999). Clearly, the second point—protecting against the unauthorized dissemination of copyrighted materials—brings us back to square one. It cannot be done feasibly without DRM technologies. At the time of this writing, the U.S. Senate has passed a bill—known as the Technology, Education, and Copyright Harmonization Act, S.487—that would extend the current copyright exemption for the classroom use of "dramatic literary and music works" (for example, movie and music clips) to distance education courses in nonprofit institutions (Carnevale, 2001b).

Institutions of higher education would be well served by faculty development programs that focus on copyright law. Institutions should also consider setting up a copyright hotline, where educators could make inquiries about the instructional use of copyrighted materials and have an answer within twenty-four hours. Such a hotline could be staffed by a resident expert on copyright law. As Bates (2000, p. 115) suggests, this person should be someone who is not afraid to exercise common sense, as "an overly rigid interpretation of the law will quickly bring all educational media production to a halt." If it has the appropriate staffing, this office could also be charged with the administrative task of requesting permissions and managing the royalty arrangements for instructional materials.

In depth education, the greatest potential for copyright infringement will be associated with the Research Libraries in each Research Center and the materials housed in the Office of the Skill Workplace. The idea centerpieces that are placed on the table in each Seminar Room of the Conference Center also have the potential for copyright infringement.

Two general rules that can help faculty and students steer clear of copyright infringements are always to request permission to use copyrighted materials (as frustrating and time consuming as this is), and to create links to Web-based materials instead of reproducing them locally. The latter can be accomplished easily with QuickPlace, with which instructors can easily develop linked pages in any knowledge room folder or embed Internet links in any document. Still, this is not a perfect solution because Web addresses change and the links may no longer be valid. In addition, much of the useful information that could be placed in the Research Center Libraries and Skill Workplace Offices will not be available on the World Wide Web.

Finally, one of the hottest topics today surrounding e-learning and copyright protection is ownership of on-line course materials and software products

(Bates, 2000; Carlson, 2000b; Carnevale and Young, 1999; Ubell, 2001). Stanley Katz (2001, p. B8) notes that one of the more troubling dimensions of the use of technology in higher education concerns the subtle transformation of professors into hired hands:

> For years, universities have asserted that processes or products patented by scientists and engineers are the intellectual property of the university, because the discoveries were made in expensive university laboratories. Faculty members have shared in the earnings of registered patents according to well-established formulas on each campus. In the past, however, faculty members were permitted, indeed encouraged, to copyright their own books and articles and to retain any profits from royalties. Now comes software for teaching that has the potential to be highly profitable. But it is also, one must say, more closely related to the teaching function for which almost all faculty members are primarily employed than to patentable research done in parts of the university. And most faculty members think that it should be treated differently.
>
> Nevertheless, the response of university administrators has been to attempt to expand the patent policy to cover such courseware, and to claim that it belongs to the university, with a profit-sharing arrangement for faculty members. In other words, for the first time, university teachers are in danger of being told that they cannot control some of the most time-consuming and creative aspects of their pedagogical duties. They are, thereby, being reconceptualized, without their consent, as workers for hire.

Although each institution has to sort out these matters on its own, the knowledge room concept tends to push the discussion in the direction of individual faculty ownership for two reasons. First, the institution makes no significant investment in the creation of knowledge rooms (unlike with an instructional CD that could cost over $100,000 to create). Second, knowledge rooms, unlike a distance education curriculum, cannot be easily abstracted from their creators; their value is derived from the teaching services offered by the educator.

Perhaps there may one day be a robust market for prefabricated knowledge rooms, each equipped with a wide range of copyrighted resources. Yet producing these turnkey knowledge room resources would be similar to writing textbooks. Most institutions would find it self-defeating to remove or share ownership rights from faculty who write books and textbooks, and the products of depth education should be seen in the same light. The first concern of college and university administrators should be to encourage faculty to be creative and innovative educators; institutional policies governing copyright ownership should serve this end.

The Library as the Campus Center

No single component of the brick-and-mortar infrastructure of colleges and universities is more important for e-learning than the library. The library is the locus of the research function of the campus and a common space for students and faculty to interact, and its staff are an important source of cross-disciplinary expertise in knowledge management.

One of the axiomatic truths confronting higher education is that the Internet is a very imperfect research tool. Although the lingua franca of the World Wide Web—hypertext markup language (HTML)—combines text and images in much the same way as the medieval scholar crafted exquisite pages (Keating and Hargitai, 1999), the resemblance stops there. Given the relative ease with which searches can be performed on the Internet, it is not surprising that students are more enthusiastic proponents of researching on the Internet than are faculty. Faculty reservations about the usefulness of the Internet as a research tool are well justified. As Carl Shapiro and Hal Varian (1999, p. 8) note,

> The fact is, the Web isn't all that impressive as an information resource. The static, publicly accessible HTML text on the Web is roughly equivalent in size to 1.5 million books. The UC Berkeley Library has 8 million volumes, and the average quality of the Berkeley library content is much, much higher! If 10 percent of the material on the Web is "useful," there are about 150,000 useful book-equivalents on it, which is about the size of a Borders superstore. But the actual figure for "useful" is probably more like 1 percent, which is 15,000 books, or half the size of an average mall bookstore.

Furthermore, most of the available Internet search engines are relatively crude instruments for focused research. This is evident to anyone who has had to wade through a multitude of irrelevant citations that are accorded high relevance by the search engine. However, this is likely to be a temporary problem. First, some search engines like Ask Jeeves (www.askjeeves.com), Google (www.google.com), and NorthernLight (www.northernlight.com) have incorporated search protocols that provide greater precision in Internet searches (Berkman, 2000; Shachtman, 1999). Second, with the development of the extensible markup language (XML) standard, which will enable a much more precise labeling of content, Internet searches will become considerably more accurate (Kiely, 1999; Marsan, 2000).

With the singular importance of libraries to academic institutions in the information age, the level of disinvestment in them is striking. This disinvestment is not the result of dwindling acquisition budgets—from 1986 through 1999 the acquisition budgets of 106 prestigious libraries belonging to the Association of Research Libraries increased by 2.3 times. Yet during this same period, the number of academic journals purchased decreased by 6 percent and the number of monographs purchased dropped by 26 percent. Much of this disinvestment is the result of the dramatic increase in the price of academic journals—by 207 percent since 1986 (Kyrillidou, 2000). Assuming an aggressive growth rate of 8 percent per year in library acquisitions, the escalating costs of academic journals, and to a lesser degree, academic monographs, means that the leading academic libraries of 2030 will have only 20 percent of the purchasing power that they had in 1980. This, of course, is to say nothing of the fiscal inability of libraries to keep up with the exponential growth of new information (Hawkins, 1998).

The Elusive Digital Library

It will be a long time before we see fully digital academic libraries. We would be lucky to see this take place within this century. Although an impressive range of academic resources are available on-line through services like EBSCO Information Services or Lexis-Nexus's Academic Universe, on-line collections of full-text journals do not make a library. As nice as it would be to come up with a technological quick fix for lowering the cost of academic journals and converting monographs to a digital format, there are several reasons to believe that this is not in the cards—at least in the foreseeable future.

First, there are real costs associated with taking archived materials and digitizing them. For example, the Cleveland Public Library contains a collection of over one million photographs. Assuming that handling and scanning each photograph takes five minutes, it would take forty years for one person to accomplish this task (Griffiths, 1998)! Although there have been remarkable advances in optical character recognition (OCR) programs, anyone who has scanned large portions of text knows how time consuming it can be. Because of the editorial time required to correct the output of even state-of-the-art high-speed scanners, commercial firms like netLibrary are resorting to the old-fashioned technology of retyping the materials they digitize—setting up outposts in China, India, and the Philippines for this purpose (Carvajal, 1999). It can cost them as much as $3,000 to digitize a book if it has many complex formulas and charts (Kiernan, 1999a). The thirty-year-old Project Gutenberg initiative, which digitizes books in the public domain, electronically publishes an average of one book a day. This sounds impressive until one realizes a single publisher, John Wiley & Sons, published more than four books a day in 1999.

Second, it is not clear that the on-line distribution of academic journals will save all that much in overall production costs. Although some promising initiatives could provide a breakthrough in academic publishing, such as the Electronic Society for Social Scientists (Payne, 2001), it is not clear that the cost savings associated with on-line publication and distribution will significantly lower the price of journal subscriptions because of the costs of maintaining a robust structure for editorial and peer review as well as copyediting and layout (Hawkins, 1998). More important, it will be some time before on-line journals match the prestige of print journals. With the exception of a few in physics, the prospects for many are dismal, owing to the difficulty of securing submissions from faculty (Kiernan, 1999b). Because much of the tenure and promotion process is focused on publication in established (that is, print) journals, junior faculty are understandably reticent to publish their work in on-line journals (Kiernan, 2000). Unlike printed journals that can be always retrieved from a library, even if the journal is discontinued, such perpetual access cannot be guaranteed to contributors of on-line journals, at least for the time being. Furthermore, although print journals are almost never read from cover to cover, faculty are much more likely to read a print article than one published on-line (Givler, 1999). Although the practice of publishing prestigious journals in both print and on-line versions will speed the acceptance of the latter, as with the *American Journal of History* (Grossberg, 2000), there are considerable costs associated with the simultaneous publication of a journal in two forms.

Third, it is likely that truly promising digital library initiatives, such as net-Library, will be hampered by the vested interests of publishers in the short term and the justifiable constraints of copyright law in the long term. netLibrary (www.netlibrary.com), a company based in Boulder, Colorado, carries more than thirty-five thousand titles in its electronic collection. Since netLibrary opened its doors on the World Wide Web in March 1999, its e-book collection has grown from two thousand titles. It has established relationships with about 210 publishers—covering trade, academic, reference, and scholarly works. The company began with 8 employees; it now has 430 (Bransten, 1999; Struckman, 2000).

When a library purchases a volume from netLibrary, it can be checked out electronically by students and faculty. Once it is checked out, it cannot be retrieved by anyone else before being checked back in. There is no significant discount associated with purchasing an on-line version of the book rather than its print version (netLibrary provides a discount of only 9 percent for volume purchases over $1 million) and netLibrary charges an additional access fee whenever a book is checked out. This fee is assessed either as a onetime payment (45 percent of the book's price) or as an annual fee (beginning at 15 percent of the book's price in the first year and declining to 3 percent in the sixth year and every year thereafter). Therefore, the savings to libraries come from not having to catalogue, house, and circulate the book, but are not related to the digital format itself (O'Leary, 1999).

In the event that netLibrary goes out of business, participating libraries would be able to secure CD-ROM versions of the texts they own (Kiernan, 1999a).

Although netLibrary seems like an idea whose time has come, the project faces three challenges. First, publishers have been reticent to release their entire line of works for digital publication, presumably because of concerns about eroding the market for their printed works. Consequently, coverage in particular subject areas tends to be spotty. However, this problem is likely to be a temporary bump in the road that will be smoothed out as publishers warm to the idea of the digital release of their work. Second, the business model used by netLibrary limits its usefulness for e-learning curricula. For example, if a course requires students to do a research project on a particular topic, students will likely be chasing after the same resources. Although schools can purchase multiple volumes of a work or professors could specify a shorter period in which the book can be checked out, e-libraries that allow for simultaneous access by multiple students, such as Questia and Ebrary, will be more useful for e-learning initiatives. The third challenge has no easy solution. It goes to the heart of research habits in academia. In netLibrary's effort to conform to U.S. copyright law, it has built in safeguards to ensure that no user will be able to copy or print more than a very modest portion of text (five thousand characters). This is considerably less than what academics are accustomed to photocopying in the normal course of research. Consequently, short of a sea change in research habits, this will likely diminish the value of netLibrary's holdings as research materials. Also, most people will find it much easier (and more satisfying) to browse through a printed book than to wade through multiple screens of on-line text—no matter which search tools become available with e-books and the increased resolution of on-line text made possible through Microsoft's ClearType or Adobe's CoolType.

Two other electronic library initiatives—Questia and Ebrary—could help warm publishers to the idea of supplying their works in digital form. Questia (www.questia.com) operates on a subscription model and is targeted for the undergraduate student who needs access to the library at 3 A.M. to complete a research paper (Blumenstyk, 2001a). Its database includes about 40,000 full-text books and journal articles in the humanities and social sciences. One nice feature of Questia's system is an automatic citation feature for generating footnotes and a bibliography. Questia also appears to have less restrictions on the ability to print documents or to copy and paste text using Windows keyboard shortcuts. Ebrary (www.ebrary.com) plans to launch an e-library initiative similar to Questia, except that patrons can read books for free and will only be charged fifteen to twenty-five cents per page when they download or print material (Carlson, 2001). The major difficulty with both of these initiatives, along with netLibrary, is the uneven coverage of their collections. Hopefully this will be resolved with time.

A Just-in-Time Solution

The aforementioned difficulties point to the need for a hybrid digital solution that takes a just-in-time approach to resource sharing among libraries. Underlying the economics of the modern academic library is a stark fact of life: only a small portion of a library's holdings actually circulates among patrons. The majority of a library's collection by far exists to handle requests from faculty and students that will likely never materialize. Although merely possessing large, uncirculating holdings may enhance the prestige of academic libraries, it is extremely inefficient.

There must be a better way for academic libraries to respond to the research needs of their respective campuses. As Martin Raish (2000) puts it, "The 'just in case' collections of the past—those that tried to anticipate users' needs by building the largest and deepest collections possible—have given way to the 'just in time' model of today: We may not have what you need right here in the building, but we can get it for you quickly." It is not surprising that interlibrary borrowing among even the most elite academic libraries has grown an average of 7.9 percent throughout the 1990s (Kyrillidou, 2000). An intentional implementation of this just-in-time model will require a more streamlined and efficient version of the interlibrary loan system that exists today.

One approach is for libraries to warehouse the books that circulate infrequently in a common location. Columbia University, the New York Public Library, and Princeton University are already using this model. Books that rarely circulate in these libraries are warehoused on Princeton's James Forrestal campus in Plainsboro, New Jersey. Initially the storage library will house seven million volumes. The facility will be expanded later to boost that capacity to thirty million. In order to put that space to best use, books and journals will be arranged by size and shape—not grouped by subject. Whenever a library patron requests a book or journal, the materials can be placed in that person's hands in twenty-four hours through a shuttle van system. If a book or journal in the storage library circulates more frequently, it can be relocated to the campus library. This system conserves precious library space while satisfying the needs of patrons to secure books and journals in a timely fashion. Jeremiah Ostriker, provost of Princeton University, observes that the number of volumes housed in the campus library has "been an area where many universities sought to compete, rather than cooperate with each other to provide the very best service for their faculty and students. I think that's an insane way to measure library strength. What you want to be able to do is to get the information on the faculty or student's desk as fast as possible" (Young, 1999b, p. A26).

Why is it not possible for libraries to pool a substantial portion of their acquisitions budget through a similar resource-sharing initiative? Instead of being

motivated by the need to free up library space (as with the Columbia–
Princeton–New York Public Library initiative), the goal of such consortiums would
be to enhance the capabilities of participating libraries to provide timely access to
library resources—not physically to possess such volumes in their stacks.[2] Co-
operative agreements between just two or three libraries could net tremendous efficiency gains. Think of the efficiency gains netted by the collaboration of five
to ten libraries!

Each consortium of libraries would run their own round-the-clock warehousing and distribution center, positioned in a geographically strategic manner.
Requests could be initiated electronically and fulfilled within a few hours. A patron could elect to pick up the book within twelve hours at the home campus library or at designated library kiosks (that is, a bank of electronic lockers that could
be secured with passwords created and e-mailed with each book order). Students could also choose to have the materials shipped directly to their home address for a nominal charge. The effect of this would be to apply the logistical
efficiencies of Amazon.com to interlibrary loan.

Although such a hybrid solution that blends aspects of digital technology with
the brick-and-mortar library may be less attractive than a hoped-for digital Library
of Alexander, it is definitely a more realistic and cost-effective alternative. It may
even be possible for colleges and universities to outsource the warehousing and
distribution functions of their libraries to private firms that see this as a market
opportunity. Furthermore, some of the increased costs associated with the collaborative warehousing of books could be recovered through the savings on classroom space brought about by depth education. This will be discussed later in
the chapter.

The biggest downside of this hybrid solution is the lack of portability—
particularly when courses are offered at several international venues. This is no
minor drawback when one considers the increased competition that residential
colleges will face in the coming years. Schools that are able to offer exotic global
venues for their programs will obviously enhance their competitive advantage.
Therefore, for the sake of portability, it is probably wise for libraries to allocate
some portion of their acquisitions budget to organizations like netLibrary.

One interesting approach would be to invite the participation of students in
the library acquisitions process by allocating a modest research budget for each
course (perhaps using a formula that ties the amount budgeted to course enrollment). For example, students could order books through accounts set up with Ama-
zon.com or another Internet bookseller. The books could be shipped directly to
them, used in the research project, and deposited in the library for cataloguing
after a prearranged time. Any quality-control difficulties that might arise could be
remedied by encouraging direct faculty oversight of the book purchases. (Ad-

mittedly, this could create a bottleneck in the system and become burdensome for educators; therefore, it would probably be used as a last resort.) It would not be a difficult matter to track these purchases so that institutions could avoid the purchase of duplicate books. These logistics could be handled completely by the Internet bookseller. If the requested book was available through netLibrary, then that bookseller could automatically purchase it from netLibrary. This approach would allow students and faculty to participate in the acquisitions process in an ongoing and timely manner through a single interface. This not only has the advantage of ensuring that the books ordered will actually be used but also gives an important feeling of empowerment to both students and faculty when it comes to the development of library resources.

Librarians as Knowledge Navigators

In addition to the investment in library acquisitions, depth education requires a greater investment in the library staff. Their campus role as knowledge navigators, promoting information literacy, will necessarily need to be strengthened. The heightened visibility of library staff is admittedly a two-edged sword. On the one hand, there will be more opportunity for library staff to interact directly with students on interesting and important research questions. Also, there will be a more compelling budget justification for increasing the size of the library staff. On the other hand, it seems likely that librarians will eventually be forced into the same round-the-clock work schedule as many of those working in IT today. Although it seems a bit incongruous to speak of a graveyard shift for research librarians, this is likely where things are heading. To the extent that librarians are the troubleshooters in their role as knowledge navigators, their services will be just as much in demand as those of computer technicians. The Library of California, a digital library created in 1998 by the State of California, is currently experimenting with round-the-clock reference services. It uses software that allows on-line librarians to see the user's screen and guide them to the most relevant information sources (Olsen, 2000a).

One promising service that would enhance the overall value of the World Wide Web as a research tool concerns the peer review of scholarly Web sites (see Gants, 1999). Research librarians working collaboratively with educators in several institutions could coordinate such an initiative. This would further reinforce the important navigational role they will hold in the information age. Already libraries at Cornell, Harvard, Johns Hopkins, and the University of California at Los Angeles are developing guidelines for judging the quality of on-line resources for academic research. In addition, the for-profit knowledge gateway Fathom.com, sponsored by Columbia University and five other institutions, features content that has passed a peer-review process (Carr and Kiernan, 2000). Just keeping up with the rising number of academic sites would be a daunting undertaking for any research library, let alone critically evaluating their content. However, a collaborative effort involving several institutions would be manageable.

The Technical Infrastructure

Although some of the infrastructure changes among faculty and library could be accomplished by reallocating current expenditures, most of the technical infrastructure for depth education will require new investment. A portion of these additional costs could be offset by savings associated with the less intensive use of classrooms (see Bleed, 2001; Carnevale, 1999a). Depending on the configuration selected by the institution or instructor, students would need to meet in a physical classroom only 25 to 33 percent of the amount of time needed to meet in traditional classroom-based instruction (for example, one hour a week for a three-credit course). The effect of this would be to increase existing classroom capacity by 200 to 300 percent. In addition, depth education does not require schools to build costly high-tech classrooms.

A key advantage of "self-service" products like QuickPlace is that they overcome the need for continuous intervention by computer professionals. This is no small benefit. Institutions of higher education must necessarily compete with corporations and government agencies to secure needed technical staff. Given the current and projected high demand for computer professionals in the corporate and government sectors, most institutions of higher education will find themselves at a disadvantage here.

Teamware is designed for the express purpose of making it easy for a non-technical person to establish and administer a secure Web space for collaborative work. Although computer professionals are needed to ensure that servers are operational and data are properly backed up, they do not have to be directly involved in setting up Web sites, assigning passwords, and posting content. In addition, teamware does not require any client programs that must be separately installed and maintained by computer support staff. All that is necessary is a Web browser and an e-mail account. This allows members of the technical staff to focus their energies on enhancing the reliability and performance of their network. In fact, smaller institutions with overburdened technical staff may want to outsource most of their network capacity allocated for e-learning, using dedicated servers from application service providers (ASPs) like Interliant or DellHost of the Dell Computer Corporation.

Computer Hardware

Much of the work to date on the technical infrastructure of college and university campuses has involved computer support for administrative functions, networking faculty computers, developing computer centers for students, and wiring the campus (for example, the library, classrooms, and dorms) for Internet connectivity. In addition, many institutions are making a significant investment in high-tech, smart classrooms that boast of videoconferencing capabilities and the full panoply of multimedia resources. The underlying assumption is that the campus is the place where technology is accessed. Although this approach fits reasonably well with undergraduate residential programs, its shortcomings become evident the further one gets from the residential model.

One of the serious drawbacks of this approach to technology is the problem of technological obsolescence. If Moore's law has taught us anything, it is that the latest and most expensive technology will always be superseded by a better and less expensive technology. Moore's law refers to an observation made in 1965 by Gordon Moore, the cofounder of Intel, who noted that the number of transistors that could be packed on a square inch of integrated circuits had doubled each year. This forecast held correct for ten years. Moore's law was revised in subsequent years to reflect a somewhat slower pace of technical change for computer chips. According to the current formulation, the processing power of computer chips will double every eighteen months.[3] The typical college or university is simply not well positioned to upgrade its technology with the rapidity needed to take advantage of these technological developments.

The core principle that should guide technology investment in higher education is that it should be in people—not real estate. This is admittedly an oversimplification. Many campuses, for example, will find the implementation of wireless technology to be a worthwhile investment (Carlson, 2000a, Olsen, 2000b). The basic idea is that schools should assume the role of technology navigators to their students and faculty.[4] In this model, institutions of higher education would focus their energies on developing technology "packages"—in collaboration with firms in the private sector—that give students and educators access to state-of-the-art computer resources. The Technology Refresh Program that links twenty-eight community colleges in Florida and the Dell Computer Corporation is a case in point (Spiwak, 2000). In this approach, the generational structure of college campuses—where a new crop of students arrives each year and another group graduates—is leveraged in order to cycle technological advances throughout the campus community. It is considerably more nimble than traditional on-campus technology investments.

The selection criteria used for putting together such technology packages should be customer support, product performance, and price—in that order. Presumably, these technology packages would most often take the form of leasing programs that accommodate the need to upgrade computers every two years or so. Because broadband Internet access could also be packaged into these leasing arrangements (as it becomes available), schools could realize substantial economic benefits from their roles as technology facilitators. The cost of each student's technology package (that is, computer hardware, software, peripherals, and broadband access) could presumably be built into the tuition and fee structure of the institution.

The dramatic price reductions in computer hardware over the past few years is obviously a great benefit in putting together technology packages that are affordable for most households. Because all students would be required to participate in the program, these concerns could be addressed through financial aid programs designed to assist those from low-income households. This is considerably fairer for such students. The laissez-faire approach toward technology that prevails on most campuses today (that is, owning your own computer is helpful but not necessary) gives a decided advantage to students who own computers. This approach also inhibits the development of computer technology in instructional settings. If students can get along without a computer, then why bother to get one? Why should faculty go to the trouble of using computers in their courses when their institutions promulgate the policy of "recommended but not required" (Bates, 2000, p. 90)?

Colleges and universities, by embracing their role as technology navigators, can focus their efforts on promoting computer skill development among students and faculty. Students, for example, could be required to participate in a sort of computer boot camp as part of their initial orientation, with follow-up skill development workshops scheduled at the beginning of each academic year. Boise State University recently put such a boot camp in place for students in its online programs with great success (Carnevale, 2000a). Also, faculty computer skills could be updated as a built-in requirement of the technology package offered by the institution. If the school assumes financial responsibility for providing faculty with computers, computer skill development workshops—held annually— would seem less like an imposition and more like an opportunity. Whenever possible, these workshops should be led by the faculty members who have been instrumental in using technology in the classroom, instead of the technical staff of the campus computing services. In this way, they help other educators to upgrade their technical skills and place the focus where it should be—on the application of digital technology to teaching (see Bates, 2000).

Network Capacity

Bandwidth and server capacity are mundane but important considerations with an application like QuickPlace. Institutions should ensure that they have ample bandwidth and server capacity to accommodate a large number of knowledge rooms and concurrent users. More important, they should have in place a plan for scaling bandwidth and server capacity upward. From the standpoint of scalability alone, many schools should take a close look at using an application service provider like DellHost or Interliant.

The adage that you can never have too much storage capacity on your PC hard drive applies to QuickPlace servers as well. "Bare bones" knowledge rooms can take anywhere from 4 MB of server space (the Portfolio Gallery) to 27.4 MB (an Assessment Suite for twenty-five students). The initial size of QuickPlace is largely determined by its number of inner rooms. For example, the Research Center only has one inner room and requires only 5.1 MB of server space. The Skill Workplace, by contrast, is an inner room intensive virtual space with a server footprint of 20.6 MB. With the dramatic increases in disk capacity (accompanied by corresponding decreases in price), QuickPlace's extensive use of storage space should not pose a problem. Moreover, the number of QuickPlaces on the server does not affect the server's performance (IBM Redbooks, 2000).

The critical factor for network capacity and the number of QuickPlace servers is the peak number of concurrent users. Because QuickPlace can be used in either an on-line or an off-line mode, the number of concurrent users will be greatly affected by the number of students who choose to work off-line. Except for those individuals who have a broadband Internet connection, students and faculty should be encouraged to take advantage of the off-line capability of QuickPlace for speed and responsiveness, regardless of whether they have a direct Internet connection at the time. The software for off-line use can be downloaded by clicking the Customize link and selecting the Off-line link. The disadvantage of off-line access is that students will not be available for an instant meeting or a brief chat. In any event, it is best to plan for more concurrent users rather than less. Furthermore, because the overall performance of QuickPlace decreases with additional concurrent users, institutions should err on the side of having more servers than fewer. There is no additional fee associated with setting up multiple QuickPlace servers.

Because QuickPlace is a processor-intensive application that scales well with additional processors, institutions should take a serious look at dual-processor servers. For example, benchmark tests on QuickPlace 2.06 indicate that a QuickPlace server operating with a single Intel 450 Mhz CPU with 512 MB RAM can accommodate 336 concurrent users in an active publishing scenario. By contrast, a dual Intel 733 MHz CPU with 512 MB RAM in an active publishing scenario will support a maximum of 1,400 concurrent users (IBM Redbooks, 2000).

Technical Support

If history is any guide, then mundane matters of technology training and general computer support will be the most significant costs in depth education. Although QuickPlace is an easy-to-use browser-based application, ample allowance must be made for hands-on training and a measure of hand-holding in making sure that people feel comfortable with the application. That said, if QuickPlace is standardized across the curriculum, the individual demand for computer support (on a per user basis) will diminish after the first month or two. Still, there would be a need for dedicated technical support to troubleshoot the sorts of problems that people inevitably have with computers.

Ultimately, there is no substitute for round-the-clock technical support for students; this is quickly becoming a baseline expectation of on-line programs (Young, 2000c). Thankfully, both computer training and support can be outsourced to some extent, but must be done with care. If schools are able to craft technology packages that provide twenty-four-hour technical support as part of the leasing arrangement, they should do so. This would allow colleges and universities to focus their efforts on other services (for example, research librarians, writing specialists) that should be provided on a round-the-clock basis.

Looking Ahead

With all the requisite caveats about predicting the future, five technological developments during the first decade of the twenty-first century will significantly enhance depth education: residential broadband Internet access, voice over IP (VOIP), near flawless voice recognition, videoconferencing, and electronic books.

Residential Broadband Internet Access

Residential broadband access to the Internet is certainly the most important of the technological developments for depth education. As discussed in Chapter 2, it may be a decade or more before we see the widespread availability of true broadband access in the 1 to 3 megabits per second range. When that becomes a reality, it will make possible a range of interesting applications, like desktop videoconferencing, integrated voice and data changes, movies and music "on demand," and the broadband virtual classroom. Perhaps more importantly, residential broadband will reinforce the ubiquity of the Internet because the connection will be "always on." Neither cable modems nor digital subscriber lines (DSL) require the standard dial-up connections to which most of us have become accustomed. In addition, a wide array of inexpensive Internet appliances and the progressive integration of wireless Internet technologies in automobiles and handheld devices will further reinforce the perception of the Internet's omnipresence.

International Data Corporation estimates that by 2003 approximately 18 million American households will access the Internet by either cable modems or DSL connections (split equally between the two). This figure represents approximately half of the 36 million American households currently connected to the Internet—of which fewer than 1.7 million currently enjoy residential broadband Internet connections (Metcalfe, 2000). Certainly the merger between America Online and Time Warner will be a factor in facilitating the growth of residential broadband, considering the 20 million subscribers to AOL and the fact that Time Warner has 65 million cable TV subscribers—not to speak of the phenomenal digital content that will be available to this $350 billion megacompany (Jones and Briody, 2000; Mehta and Chen, 2000).

In addition, developing countries will likely have greater access to the Internet with satellite technology. With the merger of ICO Global Communications and Teledesic in May 2000, the prospects for the so-called Internet-in-the-sky have brightened somewhat. Cellular phone pioneer Craig McCaw will head the new company, named ICO–Teledesic Global, based in Bellevue, Washington. Flush with a cash infusion of $1 billion from Bill Gates and others in July 2000, ICO–Teledesic Global is moving ahead with its plans to create a global network—involving 288 satellites placed in a low- earth orbit—to provide broadband Internet services (Jones, 2000). Furthermore, the joint venture between America Online and the Hughes Electronics Corporation, involving a $1.5 billion investment for the purpose of developing satellite-based Internet services, holds promise (Pasztor, 2000).[5] That said, the dot-com meltdown and cutbacks in Internet-related investment have not been kind to the Internet-based satellite projects (Pasztor, 2001).

Broadband Internet access will provide educators with a rich media environment for course development—particularly with respect to the preconfigured Research Center library resources and the office resources housed in the Skill Workplaces. These knowledge rooms could contain a vast array of media types that represent many perspectives. The video-on-demand capabilities of broadband Internet will give educators the opportunity to include expert presentations from guest speakers in their courses—the functional equivalent of providing instructors with budgets for honoraria in the magnitude of thousands of dollars! These guest speaker presentations could also be employed effectively in the Conference Center, serving as idea centerpieces for lively seminar discussions.

Voice Over IP (VOIP)

Although closely related to broadband Internet access, a technology known as voice over IP (Internet Protocol) deserves separate mention in the context of depth education. Voice over IP, or Internet telephony, refers to the use of packet-based data transmission to transmit phone calls over the Internet (Jones and Moore, 2000). The quality of Internet telephony will have to be improved before it is widely adopted, but the eventual implementation of this technology is almost inevitable for two reasons: the growing demand for unified messaging (that is, integrating e-mail, fax, and voice messages in a single inbox or data store), and the cost advantages associated with Internet-based phone calls, particularly long-distance calls over large and geographically dispersed corporate networks. It is not insignificant that Internet telephony is built into Microsoft's new Windows XP operating system (Markoff, 2001).

For depth education, voice over IP has the significant benefit of creating a seamless desktop interface that integrates audioconferencing with sharing of computer applications and data. The effect of this technology will be to render text-based chat applications obsolete. One of the first manifestations will likely be in the customer service sections of major e-commerce sites, where a customer will be able to speak directly to a service representative with a click of the mouse (Sapp, 2000; Sweat, 2000; Tillett 2000). Furthermore, the experience of seamless voice and data transmission will be greatly enhanced by the use of digital array microphones that use integrated digital signal processors to distinguish between speech and background noise. Such microphones can be placed on a monitor or beside a keyboard, permitting hands-free voice transmission—from even the distance of four to five feet—without the use of a headset or a directional microphone (Alwang, 2000).

Voice over IP will take the effort out of real-time on-line communication and mainstream use of the Internet as a conferencing tool. This will greatly facilitate the development of virtual teams and lend a more personal dimension to meetings in virtual space.

Voice Recognition

Although voice over IP will make real-time communication effortless, most of the interactions in knowledge rooms are asynchronous—that is, anytime, anywhere. This currently requires faculty and students to interact through their keyboards—a source of weariness for all concerned. Imagine, for example, being forced to convert into text all of your lectures, every parenthetical comment made in class, and every response to a student's question. Few would find teaching a gratifying experience under these circumstances! Students are equally hampered in this environment, particularly if they are not proficient typists.

Thankfully, the outlook for voice recognition is so bright that this will be a short-lived problem for e-learning. Over the past two years software programs devoted to voice recognition—like Naturally Speaking from DragonSystems or ViaVoice from IBM—have made remarkable advances (Fallows, 2000). In 1999, the accuracy of these programs hovered between 96 and 98 percent (or twenty to forty errors per one thousand words) as compared with accuracy rates of 90 percent in 1998. It will not be long before the effective accuracy of such programs will reach 99 percent (Alwang, 1999). Such near flawless voice recognition, combined with the use of digital array microphones, will be a tremendous boon for e-learning. Breaking the keyboard barrier will also facilitate more comprehensive faculty evaluations of student work and student evaluations of other students' work.

Videoconferencing

Videoconferencing will increase the richness of depth education's one-on-one or small group on-line interactions. This will replicate some of the dimensionality of face-to-face communication.[6] Later, when the next generation of the Internet—Internet2 (see www.internet2.edu)—becomes widely available, the quality of videoconferencing will be so improved that it may be possible to substitute videoconferencing for the classroom component of depth education. This assumes a class size in the neighborhood of seven to twelve students. Even so, the high caliber of videoconferencing applications made possible by the super-bandwidth capabilities of Internet2 (approximately forty-five thousand times as fast as a typical modem) will be unable to replicate every aspect of face-to-face interaction.

The one big problem with the widespread use of videoconferencing is vanity. Most people do not feel that the camera does them justice. The poor lighting associated with most home work spaces will surely not enhance a person's attractiveness. Furthermore, the lack of direct eye contact and the diminished opportunity for gesture-based communication make videoconferencing a second-best option when compared to face-to-face interactions. The bottom line is that one needs a compelling logistical or economic rationale to do away with the brick-and-mortar classroom completely. Yet despite its drawbacks, videoconferencing is likely to revolutionize how we communicate in virtual spaces, particularly in the workplace contexts of virtual teams and telecommuting.

Electronic Books

It is difficult to evaluate the prospects of electronic books at this time. On the one hand, e-books hold great potential in providing a workable solution for copyright protection (Weber, 2000b). On the other hand, it is difficult to understand how people will ever get used to reading major portions of text from a small screen (Ditlea, 2000). It is likely that e-books will not really take off until revolutionary, low-cost displays are available, in the next five years or so, which will make it possible to roll up a computer display like a piece of paper (Jefferson, 2000).

The main payoff of e-books has to do with their impact on the publishing industry. Textbook publishers have a strong financial incentive to develop the market for e-books because of the declining revenue due to the market for used textbooks. An instructor could mix and match sections of two or three separate texts into a coherent single text that could be "printed" at virtually no cost. Such flexible texts will offer a far more rational way to market textbooks than the costly current system of dangling "free" examination texts in front of faculty in the hope that someone will bite. Assuming that a workable solution will be found for the copyright protection of digital files, the content produced for e-texts could be readily integrated within the knowledge room framework of depth education—especially within the Research Library of the Research Center or the Office of the Skill Workplace.

Font-enhancement technologies like Microsoft's ClearType and Adobe's CoolType will facilitate the acceptance of digital texts (Clark, 1999; Levin 2000; Wingfield, 2000). These technologies increase the resolution of text displayed on LCD screens—the screens found on laptops, flat panel computer displays, and electronic books.[7] Currently, reading a book on a computer display may be likened to wading through a thick printout from an early dot-matrix printer. Both Microsoft's ClearType and Adobe's CoolType use a technique known as *color anti-aliasing* to boost the resolution of screen text by 300 percent. Each pixel (the smallest element of an image that can be programmed in a video display) is made up of three elements: red, green, and blue light. These color elements can be adjusted to provide the millions of colors that make photorealistic computer displays possible. The basic idea behind ClearType and CoolType is to treat each of these color elements as a separate pixel—the effect being that jaggedness of computer text is smoothed out. Consequently, screen text is almost as clear as text in printed books, thereby reducing eyestrain.

We are now ready to explore some exciting avenues of service for higher education in the twenty-first century.

CHAPTER FIVE

NEW HORIZONS
FOR HIGHER EDUCATION

The twenty-first century is a time of unparalleled promise for higher education. Mass-produced distance education will open up new knowledge horizons for millions of people who otherwise would have no opportunity to attend a college or university, and blended approaches to e-learning will enrich classroom-based education. It would be difficult to imagine a more creative and rewarding era for educators.

In this new academic era, educators have a profound responsibility to champion and model the core ethical values that underlie academic inquiry, such as respecting differences, upholding the freedom of inquiry, and valuing dialogue and debate. These values—essentially democratic in character—must not be buried in the fine print of academic inquiry but instead held up with pride. One place to start recovering the ethical moorings of higher education is in the classroom. Teaching is not simply a means for faculty to conduct research. Rather, it is the work of awakening others from the deep slumber of unchallenged assumptions and unrealized potential. There is no higher calling than this.

The ethical character of higher education should also permeate the organizational culture of the academy. Robust communities of inquiry that make education an exciting experience for both students and educators can hardly take root in organizational cultures marked by isolation, fear, territoriality, and power plays. If full-time faculty fail in something as basic as defending the academic freedom of their adjunct colleagues, what hope is there for the educational enterprise?

Graduate students should not be treated like colleagues-in-waiting but rather respected as full partners in academic inquiry. Undergraduates are not simply a means to pay the bills but rather the raison d'être of higher education.

One of the great social missions of higher education will be to bridge the digital divide. Because e-learning is destined to be one of the "killer apps" of this century, it provides a sort of grand justification for extending Internet access to marginalized people and isolated communities. The convergence of political, social, and economic forces that will extend it into the far reaches of the planet will ultimately make the digital divide a historical relic. There is some evidence that this is already happening in the United States. Although the digital divide is still a reality in America, the gap between high- and low-income households appears to be narrowing. A recent study by the Pew Internet and American Life Project found that 38 percent of adults in households making less than $30,000 per year had Internet access, as compared with 28 percent just six months earlier. While the digital divide is also evident in comparing Internet use between white adults and black or Hispanic adults, the gap seems to be narrowing. Forty-three percent of black adults indicated that they have gone on-line in November and December 2000 as compared to 35 percent just six months previously. Among Hispanic adults, 47 percent reported that they had gone on-line in November and December 2000 as compared to 40 percent in May and June 2000 (Grenier, 2001). It may not be before midcentury that the digital divide between the less and more developed worlds is bridged, and it may take even longer to remove socioeconomic barriers to information access in developing countries, but the gap between the digital have's and have-not's will eventually be bridged.

That said, status distinctions will always persist. The speed and quality of Internet access will become a significant equal-opportunity issue. Mass-produced distance education will naturally be seen as less valuable than the more faculty-intensive, blended varieties of e-learning, just as there are status distinctions currently between private and public education, four-year institutions and community colleges, liberal arts curricula and professional programs, and top-tier schools and all the others. The fabulous bargain of the Internet age is that we can substitute distinctions like these for the widespread inaccessibility of higher education across the planet.

The International Distributed Campus

Although most educational institutions have no chance of achieving the distinction of global university (discussed in Chapter Two), many institutions could reconfigure themselves as internationally distributed campuses, using the knowledge room framework and a blended approach to e-learning. This would be a tremendous contribution to learning worldwide. Also the international distributed campus would likely be able to find the economic means to sustain itself in the competitive framework of mass-produced distance education.

The international distributed campus would work like this. A college or university in a more developed country could establish a presence in one or two locations in the developing world. It could develop a nontraditional campus (perhaps in collaboration with a local, sister institution) in a hotel or other building complex, consisting primarily of guest rooms wired for the Internet and conference space for classes. Students from the institution's home campus could spend two or more terms at these satellite campuses—perhaps a required international experience during their first two years and an elective experience during their junior or senior years.

Most students at these international locations would live in the vicinity. Because the logistics of transportation in many large urban centers in developing countries are daunting, the school could establish several Internet cafés strategically positioned around the city. Students who could not access the Internet from home would be able to do their work at these centers. Once a week, they could travel to the hotel residence–classroom center for face-to-face interactions with their professors and with the students visiting from the home campus.

Could an arrangement like this be sustainable from a financial standpoint? Answering this question requires careful consideration of the local infrastructure, governmental regulation, local education markets, transportation logistics, political stability, and exchange rate fluctuations. It can only be answered on a case-by-case basis. Given these qualifications, though, one suspects that such initiatives hold the potential for being highly profitable. There is such pent-up demand for high-quality education in the developing world. Students around the world are eager to invest in their futures and will gladly pay more for a high-quality education that prepares them for the twenty-first-century workplace. Even if low-cost, mass-produced distance education is available, most students will cherish more interaction with their teachers and the opportunity to develop meaningful friendships with visiting students. Also, employers will certainly understand the value of an education that is built around the virtual team concept and emphasizes knowledge management.

In addition to the immediate financial benefits, the international distributed campus would provide the home campus with a great educational payoff. The cross-cultural interactions made possible by an institution's satellite programs not only bring perspective and dimensionality to the learning experiences of students but also enrich the teaching experiences of faculty. These cross-cultural benefits could be enhanced if students from developing countries were encouraged to make regular electronic visits to the home campus, perhaps serving as guest participants in a seminar discussion or as respondents to a research project.

The intergenerational character of depth education brings another benefit to the international distributed campus. For example, a retired CEO could participate in a course on leadership or organizational behavior taking place on the other side of the world—while enjoying a morning cup of coffee. This would be a tremendous avenue of service! With the changing demographics of the industrialized world, the services provided by highly qualified retired professionals could have a life-changing impact on all concerned.

Downstream Educational Services

One of the important secondary benefits of e-learning is an institution's enhanced ability to develop a range of downstream alumni services. Most colleges and universities do little more than hold out their hands to their graduates—setting aside homecoming rituals and granting preferential treatment in the application process for children of alumni. Schools that walk away from this "give me" orientation and offer valuable downstream services will not only add value to their degrees but also invest in the intellectual capital of their alumni community. This approach is already in evidence at Harvard, Northwestern, Princeton, Stanford, the University of North Carolina at Chapel Hill, Yale, and other schools ("Harvard to Offer Minicourses," 2001; Leibowitz, 1999; Carr, 2000j).

The most useful postgraduate service offered by institutions of higher education comes though the career counseling and placement office. However, such career-focused services play a very brief role in a graduate's career and therefore have little overall value. This is particularly true in economies that require individuals to pursue many different careers during their adult lives. Even notable initiatives like educational guarantees—for example, refunding tuition to students who are unable to secure employment in some predetermined period after graduation—have little relevance one or two years after graduation.

The strategic goal of any downstream service is to extend, and wherever possible, increase the value of those services over time. Five downstream services, in particular, are promising for institutions of higher education: credentialing services, networking services, self-confidence services, mentoring services, and portfolio services. What is notable about top-tier institutions is that they excel in their credentialing services and have a strong record of performance in both networking and self-confidence services. Their strength in these three areas is so valuable that they are assured of maintaining their commanding position in the educational marketplace.

Credentialing Services

Currently the most significant downstream service of colleges and universities has to do with the credential value of their degrees in the marketplace. As one would expect, this value varies markedly, depending on the reputation of the school and the relative worth of the degree in the labor market. It is equally clear—bringing in the dimension of time—that the value of academic credentials (compared to other factors such as work experience) declines steadily as distance from graduation increases. It should be noted, however, that credentialing services are often linked to networking services—particularly in the case of top-tier schools. Because the value of networking services often increases over time, this gives a credential a measure of value that remains stable, or even appears to grow, with the passage of time.

A recent study has called into question that a degree from an Ivy League institution yields a bona fide economic payoff for its graduates, particularly when the earnings of top-tier graduates are compared with those of students who were admitted to Ivy League institutions but chose to go elsewhere (Gose, 2000b). Several factors could explain this, including the increased attention that top students receive from professors at less selective institutions. Still the perception that an Ivy League degree is something of great value will be with us for a long time, due primarily to the associated networking opportunities available to graduates throughout their careers. In fact, the value of these downstream services is so great that top-tier schools may even be tempted to auction off a portion of classroom seats to the highest bidder—irrespective of academic merit. Georgetown University is currently experimenting with auctioning three of sixteen seats in a *certificate* multimedia program ("Georgetown University Turns to Virtual Auctioneer," 2000). One can only hope that top-tier schools will not resort to such measures for their bona fide degree programs, but the point is that they could do so with great success if they wanted to because of the perceived value downstream of their degrees.[1]

Networking Services

Networking services, when they are effectively used, give graduates significant advantages in the labor market. These services should not be understood restrictively as developing contacts or getting inside information about a particular position. Networking, in the sense used here, means being part of a larger support structure that enhances a graduate's chance of success—however that may be defined.

The value of any network will be related to its size and the commitment or loyalty invested in that network by its participants. As to the size of the network, there is a well-known principle in computer circles known as Metcalfe's law, postulated in the late 1970s by Bob Metcalfe, the inventor of the Ethernet technology for computer networking. This principle holds that the value of a network is equal to its numbers of users squared ($v = n^2$, where v is the value of the network and n is the number of users). The value, for example, of an eBay auction for buyer and seller will be considerably different if there are 10,000 registered users of eBay instead of 22.5 million. Obviously, schools that have been around for one to two centuries and have fielded many graduates will enjoy a networking advantage over those with less longevity and fewer graduates.

But size is not the only consideration. If that were the case, then a large state school could offer its graduates a more valuable network than an Ivy League school. Commitment is a considerably more potent factor than size in the value of networks. Small networks with remarkably high commitment can be forces to be reckoned with; the Mafia offers a classic example. If individuals freely invest a significant portion of their identity in a network, that is a sure sign that its members expect some tangible or intangible benefit. Otherwise, why should they invest themselves in it in the first place?

As with credentialing services, top-tier institutions have performed the best in this area because they have been able to credibly convey the message to students and alumni that they are lifetime members of an elite club. The benefit of being part of an elite network is that participants are conferred a presumption of familiarity due to their affiliation with the school. Such ascribed familiarity opens doors to social interactions and job interviews that might otherwise remain closed. The esprit de corps of the alumni networks of top-tier schools is constantly reinforced in ways that are both subtle and overt. Even a ritual as institutionally self-serving as a capital campaign allows these institutions to remind alumni of their privileged status, as evidenced by their worldly success, and their responsibility to help perpetuate this tradition for future generations.

Schools below the top tier have great opportunities to use Internet technology to enhance the value of their alumni networks. For example, the development of industry-specific career convention centers on the Internet, where alumni share career development information and provide mentoring support, could be of tremendous value. For schools that focus on values or religion, such convention centers could be extended to a number of other arenas beyond career development, including parenting, social justice advocacy, and other concerns.

Self-Confidence Services

Self-confidence is probably the most valuable asset that institutions of higher education can give to their students. The value of credentials and network access pales in comparison. Having the self-confidence to navigate social networks, explore unfamiliar territory, and tackle difficult problems is of immense value. Although self-confidence can be nourished in many ways, the experience of challenge is critical. It is almost immaterial whether the challenge is physical, intellectual, or social. People gain self-confidence by taking on a challenge, meeting failure, picking themselves up, and trying again—eventually being successful and finding new challenges to tackle.

As with credentialing and networking services, top-tier institutions have been generally successful in cultivating self-confidence in their students and alumni, primarily by reinforcing the idea that those who walk their halls make up an exclusive, "chosen" group. Although every school uses the pomp and circumstance of commencement exercises to impart the sense that their students are joining an elite host of graduates, only top-tier institutions have the social credibility to make that belief stick after the last graduation party breaks up. Winning admission to a top-tier institution is itself a tremendous boon to a young person's self-confidence, given the odds that applicants face. For example, in 1999 both Harvard and Columbia rejected nine out of every ten applicants (Steinberg, 2000b). This says nothing about the cumulative weight of positive academic experiences and social advantages that build toward the acceptance letter. Zachary Karabell (1998, p. 198) puts it in this way:

> Students at elite schools are not necessarily smarter than students at less selective schools, but they do have several advantages. Not only are they more affluent, they also have had better secondary educations, and they arrive at places like Stanford and Georgetown secure in their ability to learn new material. They think they're smart, and they're not afraid to speak about things that they don't know much about. . . . But students who take a night course at a local college are less likely to be convinced of their brilliance. On the contrary, they often lack self-confidence in their abilities, and this makes it hard for them to work their way through difficult ideas and concepts. Not because they can't but rather because they don't believe they can.

Unlike prestige-based credentialing and networking services, top-tier schools do not enjoy a monopolistic advantage when it comes to imparting self-confidence to their students—particularly when self-confidence is nurtured for reasons other than exclusivity. Unfortunately, schools outside the top-tier have not done a very good job in this area because students are largely denied the experience of being challenged. One suspects that the commoditization of instruction is largely to blame. Commoditization, discussed earlier in the book, rewards sameness in structure and content, as well as similarity of outcomes (for example, grade distributions skewed to provide the illusion of content and skill mastery). Students are socialized into a kind of force-feeding process where the operative rules for success are to sit, try to be attentive, and make sure they know what is going to be on the test. Information is here today and gone tomorrow.

Any real challenge is missing from the typical classroom. How is it possible to create challenging educational environments if learning is reduced to a set of information transactions? The lack of meaningful challenge in high school is also to blame. How many promising students have been disabled before walking into a college classroom because no one bothered to ask them "to let their reach exceed their grasp," as the old maxim goes?

The problem-solving framework of depth education goes a long way toward remedying the lack of meaningful challenge in the classroom. Also, the geographic flexibility that e-learning makes possible can be put to good advantage when it comes to providing students with rich experiences. The cross-cultural experiences associated with the international distributed campus could be of great help in the formation of self-confidence.

Self-confidence services for alumni would likely focus on developing a new genre of continuing education courses for them. These courses could focus on introducing alumni to cutting-edge knowledge domains or skills.[2] One could imagine many directions that next-generation continuing education courses could take. For instance, genetic science is poised to make tremendous advances in the coming years, yet knowledge of this field among most educated people is limited to Mendel's seeds and vague recollections of the building blocks of DNA strands. Although no continuing education course will turn people into geneticists, it could impart enough information to help them better understand the social and ethical impact of everything from the Human Genome Project to Dolly the sheep.

The same holds true for knowledge domains that will have tremendous social and economic impact in the coming years, such as virtual reality technologies and telecommunications. New skill sets are constantly emerging on the widening horizon of technological developments. For example, how will the increased use of electronic conferencing transform our understanding of negotiating skills? What skills and strategies are necessary to safeguard privacy in the face of expanding electronic transactions and Internet insecurity? Through such continuing education programs, institutions of higher education would cultivate a culture of exploration and discovery among their alumni, emphasizing the point that no knowledge domain or skill set is beyond their reach.

Mentoring Services

One of the least understood facets of education is the degree to which certain teachers can make a lasting impression on their students. Interactions that may seem fleeting or inconsequential at the time are cherished for a lifetime. Take the case of

Jerome Kagan, a distinguished child psychologist. His interest in psychology came about after a professor made an idle comment during a course in introductory psychology. "He had posed a question I cannot remember, but to which I apparently gave a good answer. He asked me to stay and as we walked across the campus he said I had an apperceptive feeling for psychology and added, 'You would probably be a good psychologist.' The sentence rings as clearly now as it did that afternoon 22 years ago" (Pillemer, Picariello, Law, and Reichman, 1996, p. 319).

If it were possible to duplicate such teacher-student interactions and facilitate the development of lifelong mentoring relationships between faculty and their former students, this would be a wonderful educational service. Unfortunately, that is not possible. Such moments cannot be manufactured but proceed from the serendipity of human relationships. Besides emphasizing the overall accessibility of faculty to alumni through e-mail exchanges and school-sponsored social gatherings, it is likely that little can be done at the institutional level to encourage mentoring relationships after graduation.

That said, colleges and universities are well positioned to offer two mentoring services that address the increasing need for sound career advice after graduation: credential counseling services and vocational development services. The credential counseling service could be offered by faculty mentors; the vocational development service could enlist more experienced alumni.

Credential counseling services will grow increasingly important in the New Economy as college alumni need to think strategically about a range of educational alternatives when they retool for new careers. Often people make significant investments in graduate education without the benefit of up-to-date information about educational alternatives from a disinterested party. Graduate admissions counselors and program directors are in no position to offer such counsel. Colleges and universities could help meet this need by offering educators incentives to specialize in specific areas of the labor market and to be well informed about the strengths and weaknesses of different credential options in particular job categories. Alumni who are planning to work on an advanced degree or certification program could contact a designated faculty member specializing in the vocational area of their choice. If such degree or certification programs are offered by the institution itself, the faculty mentors would have to offer accurate and disinterested advice—not promote the advantages of their own programs.

Vocational development services focus on helping alumni advance in their careers, not on retooling for a new vocation. Although many educators can play a useful role here, there is no doubt that established alumni who are working in that area are in a much better position to be helpful. For example, one or two established alumni could host an ongoing electronic conference for alumni who are beginning careers in a specific field.

Portfolio Services[3]

Institutions of higher education have a tremendous opportunity to offer electronic portfolio services that spotlight significant achievements in the working careers of alumni. Educational institutions are uniquely situated to offer such services; companies have no vested interest in drawing attention to the marketability of their employees. These electronic portfolios would be more than enhanced digital resumes. Such services would provide alumni with a self-service venue for collecting in-depth and concrete examples of their workplace achievements.

The knowledge room framework of depth education provides an ideal environment in which to develop on-line career portfolios—particularly in the context of graduate programs. Students could begin work on these portfolios early in their program, with portfolio projects woven into the curriculum. By the time a student graduates, he or she would be able to exhibit a rich set of career-enhancing outcomes and experiences. These portfolios could be periodically updated by alumni to reflect their expanding competencies and major achievements.[4] The value in these portfolios may have little to do with the process of securing employment; their effect on strengthening self-confidence and facilitating periodic career counseling could be much more valuable.

Upstream Educational Services

Although colleges and universities can add value to their educational programs by offering all these downstream services, the social impact of these initiatives pales in comparison to upstream educational initiatives for high-school-age students. There is a tremendous market opportunity here for institutions of higher education—and a redemptive social mission.

As an institution of learning, the high school is a comparatively young innovation. Although the first public high school in the United States opened its doors in Boston in 1821, it was not until 1933 that most American youth were enrolled (a result of the unavailability of work during the Great Depression). Following World War II, Americans adopted the belief that high school education should be available to all.

What is striking about the institution of high school during the second half of the twentieth century is its social success in segregating American youth from older members of the society. Although the term *teenager* was coined anonymously in 1940, the development of the teenager concept, and the commercial trappings that have gone along with it, began with the universalization of the high school experience in the 1950s. This ghettoization of American young people, reinforced by afterschool work routines in workplaces where teens dominate (fast food, mall shops, and so on), has meant that teens, by default, take their behavioral cues from other teens. Of course, the mass media has also done its part to promote teen culture in the United States for obvious commercial reasons (see Hine, 1999; National Public Radio, 1999).

One cannot survey the educational landscape in America without a profound sense of distress about the institution of high school. Sixty percent of high school seniors confess to spending less than six hours a week on homework, and a record number of seniors are signing up for advance placement courses because they find their courses so unchallenging (Kronholz, 1999). A survey of more than twenty thousand American high school students found that 40 percent were disengaged from the educational process and just going through motions (25 percent report that they never read). Yet most of these will have no difficulty getting into college—a warm body is all that is needed (Toby, 2000).

The preliminary report by the National Commission on the High School Senior Year (2001), appointed by the U.S. Department of Education, characterized the senior year of high school as "a lost opportunity": "Senior year becomes party-time rather than a time to prepare for one of their most important life transitions. Students are bored and studying becomes irrelevant. . . . Many students reported 'ditching' senior classes because the atmosphere encouraged them to consider the senior year a farewell tour of adolescence and school" (pp. 15–17). The Commission found that a number of graduates found their high school curriculum to be pointless and boring. One student put it like this: "People who graduate from high school generally spend half of their high school career asleep or dreaming. So there's no wonder when high school graduates go to college or directly to work they know next to nothing" (p. 18).

The Third International Mathematics and Science Study provides compelling evidence of the problem we face. The study was the most comprehensive of its kind, covering forty-one countries, and it compared student achievement in mathematics and science in fourth grade, eighth grade, and the final year of secondary school. In the United States alone, over thirty-three thousand students drawn from more than five hundred public and private schools were involved. The study found that in the fourth grade, U.S. students scored above the international average in both mathematics and science. By the eighth grade, they were above the international average in science but had fallen below the average in mathematics. By the final year of secondary education, U.S. students scored near the bottom of all participating countries in both science and mathematics—even those students considered the most advanced. Only the composite performance of students from South Africa and Cyprus were below that of U.S. twelfth-grade students (U.S. Department of Education, 1999).

What explains such dismal performance in the high school years? It is difficult to escape the conclusion that high school is a place where, for many students, interest in learning dies. This is not to issue a blanket condemnation of all high schools; not a few are committed to excellence and innovation. That said, most redeeming qualities of high school are found outside of the academic curriculum. Although there is certainly great value in extracurricular activities during the high school years, particularly when it comes to building self-confidence, students who are marginalized by cliquish groups or simply adolescent clumsiness are denied even this social benefit.

There are immense opportunity costs (that is, costs associated with forgone alternatives) associated with the high school experience in America. There is not only the risk of losing a child to drugs or a moment of madness such as the one at Columbine but also the absence of meaningful intellectual challenge in the typical high school classroom. High school jeopardizes personal growth by forcing young people into a one-size-fits-all pattern—based on chronology rather than ability or interest—that far too often ends in a downward spiral. Those who excuse the academic shortcomings of secondary education often point to the redeeming social lessons of the high school experience—like learning to live in the real world. One must ask, though, what is this real world? If it is the workplace of adults, then there are good reasons to doubt that high school provides much preparation. For example, behaviors that are often winked at in many high school classrooms—like inattentiveness, disrespect, and even sexual harassment—would not be tolerated in a normal workplace setting. How, then, is high school good preparation for the real world?

E-learning provides colleges and universities with an educational delivery system that can rescue young minds from the boredom of the high school classroom while allowing young people the opportunity to maintain their circle of friends, and whenever possible, participate in the extracurricular activities offered by high school. Although one can make a good case that serious sixteen-year-old students can thrive on a college campus and successfully navigate its curriculum, it is unrealistic to think that most parents will consent to such a dramatic paradigm shift. Virtual high school programs are already being developed at the University of Nebraska, Indiana University, the University of Missouri, Lehigh University, Michigan State University, and the University of California (Carr and Young, 1999; Carr, 1999c, 2000i). Furthermore, on-line preparation courses for college admissions, like those of the Kaplan Educational Centers, will help acquaint high school students and their parents with the benefits of e-learning (Gose, 2000a).

Despite the flurry of activity surrounding virtual high school programs, one wonders if it is realistic to expect high school students to be motivated enough to participate in a standard distance education format. The early results from on-line advanced placement courses are not encouraging. For example, during the 1999–2000 academic year, only one-third of the six hundred students who enrolled in the advanced placement courses offered by Apex Learning of Bellevue, Washington, actually completed their course work (Steinberg, 2000a). Some hybrid solution that combines e-learning with face-to-face interaction will likely be necessary. What would such a hybrid program look like?

First, it would have to incorporate the services of well-prepared and mature undergraduates as TAs. This not only would counteract the ghettoization of teenagers and have a positive modeling effect but also would make possible the development of teaching fellowship programs at the undergraduate level. Simply replacing high school teachers with college professors is not a viable solution.

Second, such programs would have to include initiatives designed to incorporate high school students into a community of inquiry. Although the virtual team format of depth education will be helpful in this regard, students will also need to meet in person for two or three days at a time at regular intervals. This could be done through the development of regional minicampuses (such as hotels or retreat centers) that serve as biweekly gathering points for enrolled students to meet with faculty members and teaching assistants. The curriculum could also make good use of summer travel programs, and perhaps even more extensive, semesterlong cross-cultural experiences.

Third, it is likely that the current system of advance placement courses will become irrelevant. According to Roger Schank (2000), "Eventually it will be possible to take an entire first year of college in high school and receive college credit. Once this happens, the AP system as we know it will disappear. There will be no need to have an arbitrary test determine whether or not students get credit for a course. They will take the same course college freshmen are taking and get college credit directly" (p. 45).

The ultimate benefit of such upstream initiatives goes far beyond providing young people with the equivalent of one or two years of college-level work by their eighteenth birthday, or reducing the residential costs of attending college. The real benefit is in the number of young people who may be freed from the debilitating effects of boredom and discover (or rediscover) the value of intellectual curiosity.

Wisdom: Higher Education's Great Frontier

"Wonder is the feeling of the philosopher, and philosophy begins in wonder" (Plato, *Theaetetus*, Sec. 155). These words, attributed to Socrates, capture the essential relationship between curiosity and critical reflection. Exploration and discovery lie at the base of every human achievement and aspiration. The knowledge that leads to wisdom opens new vistas and discloses how little we really do know. Wisdom suffers no pretense that one has arrived. Knowledge can be mastered, but wisdom can only be sought. Wisdom both proceeds from knowledge and transcends it, favoring the elegance of simplicity over erudition. Wisdom illuminates what is important in a knowledge landscape, penetrating to "the core of what really matters" (Allee, 1997, p. 44).

Wisdom may be understood as the most durable kind of knowledge, moving beyond the confines of *how* to *why* (Pelikan, 1992). Most people have an intuitive sense of the limits of knowledge when it comes to important life decisions that require the counsel of others and wisdom. Aristotle, in his *Nicomachean Ethics* (Book Six, Chapter Seven), described wisdom as the most precise and perfect form of knowledge. Wisdom is more easily apprehended than defined; those who encounter it understand its value and immediately accord it respect. The capability that enables people to deliberate well—what Aristotle called practical wisdom—is strongly tied to the attribute of discernment. The ability to filter the important from the insignificant, to perceive worth among the ordinary, to hear a voice of authenticity above the background noise—these are qualities of the wise. Yet knowledge and wisdom are closely related. Wisdom nearly always issues from perceptive observation and reflection on everyday life or the in-depth application of knowledge. Both the learned and the unlearned can be wise, but not the ignorant.

Higher education can have no higher calling than to create learning environments that inspire wonder. Wisdom cannot be programmed into a curriculum or delivered as an educational outcome. But it is possible to create learning contexts that are conducive to development of wisdom. Such "wisdom-friendly" learning environments would provide students with many opportunities to reflect on how the possession of knowledge creates new responsibilities to use it well. The ancient truth that knowledge imparts responsibility—"to whom much is given, of him will much be required" (Luke 12:48)—could not have greater relevance in the classrooms of our day.

In effect, wisdom poses the ultimate "so what" question. Why is knowledge important? Toward what end does the pursuit of knowledge aspire? What is our response to knowledge? From the constructivist standpoint, all knowledge is constructed from the interplay between experience and one's own cognitive templates (including individual and social values). Responding to what we know, therefore, always involves an internal dialogue about not only the limitations of knowledge but also its possibilities. Knowing, in this sense, constitutes an invitation to ethical inquiry, given the pronounced role of individual and social values in shaping our understanding of the world.

Although institutions of higher education cannot deliver or certify wisdom in any sense, they can provide students with ample opportunity to reflect on the larger meaning and significance of their encounters with new knowledge. This process of reflection about knowledge must not be confined to courses in the humanities; it should be incorporated across the curriculum.

In depth education, such opportunities for reflection can be incorporated in all knowledge rooms. For example, students could be asked in the Research Center to go beyond their findings to reflect on how their research shaped their own attitudes or beliefs or to track the implications of their research for public policy. Similarly, students working in the Skill Workplace might be asked to reflect on how their own core values influenced the way they applied a new skill to a case study. Perhaps the Conference Room is the most natural venue for such ethical reflection. During the give-and-take of individual seminars, professors can not only ask students to offer their opinions on certain questions but also engage them in an analysis of the factors and values that shape those opinions. Such exercises in critical awareness transform free-form discussions into opportunities for self-examination and dialogue about larger ethical issues and questions of meaning. A similar approach could be taken in the Debate Hall by asking students to publish a brief ethical reflection on the debate, particularly highlighting the ethical weaknesses of the positions they advocated during it. Finally, in the Portfolio Gallery students could be asked to reflect on the artistic dimensions of the project and how these might shape their overall vision.

Although the knowledge room framework offers students many opportunities to reflect on their own responses to new knowledge, there is no better place for such interaction than the brick-and-mortar classroom. In depth education, the classroom is not the place to transmit information but rather to provoke dissent, nurture rapport and collegiality, and light the fires of curiosity and the passion for inquiry.

Once the classroom is declared a sacred space for reflecting on and grappling with new knowledge—instead of serving as a loading dock where information is conveniently laid out for distribution—a new set of expectations for classroom interaction will evolve. There is no reason why the classroom cannot become a dedicated instrument for discovery and discernment, creating an intellectual atmosphere where the knowledge that leads to wisdom can flourish. No greater gift could be offered to students than this. Nothing in higher education could be more rewarding.

NOTES

Chapter 1

1. Much of this discussion relies on Fosnot's (1996, see pp. 8–33) excellent summary of constructivism.

2. It is often assumed that constructivism requires one to adopt a position of relativism in relation to truth claims (because all knowledge is individually constructed). This is not necessarily the case. One could, for example, apply some criterion of viability to distinguish between knowledge claims that are underdeveloped or spurious and those that stand the test of time (Jonassen, Peck, and Wilson, 1998). One could also posit some criterion of adequacy built on Vygotsky's (1986) distinction between spontaneous and scientific concepts— that is, the attraction of spontaneous concepts to scientific ones suggests that the latter are more adequate than the former.

3. The concept of deep learning finds its roots in British perspectives on education, in contrast to the survey-oriented or surface approach taken by many American educators (see Marchese, 1997). Some of the key aspects of the depth education model presented here have been expressed in recent essays by Bothun (1999), Frayer (1999), Gilbert (2000), and Talbott (1999).

4. The concept of scaffolding was introduced by David Wood, Jerome Bruner, and Gail Ross (1976, p. 90): "Discussions of problem solving or skill acquisition are usually premised on the assumption that the learner is alone and unassisted. If the social context is taken into account, it is usually treated as an instance of modeling and imitation. But the intervention of a tutor may involve much more than this. More often than not, it involves a kind of 'scaffolding' process that enables a child or novice to solve a problem, carry out a task or achieve a goal which would be beyond his unassisted efforts. This scaffolding consists

essentially of the adult 'controlling' those elements of the task that are initially beyond the learner's capacity, thus permitting him to concentrate upon and complete only those elements that are within his range of competence. The task thus proceeds to a successful conclusion. We assume, however, that the process can potentially achieve much more for the learner than an assisted completion of the task. It may result, eventually, in the development of task competence by the learner at a pace that would far outstrip his unassisted efforts."

5. The problem with interpreting lecture notes as theft of intellectual property is that they are necessarily interpretations of the instructor's material (see Olsen, 1999). This is akin to a group of students pooling their resources and creating a study guide that is photocopied and distributed in preparation for an exam. The unauthorized use of taping and transcribing lectures and posting them to the Internet would be a different story.

6. Harasim, Hiltz, Teles, and Turnoff (1995, p. 167) expressed this concept in the following manner: "In keeping with a learner-centered approach, evaluation and assessment should be part of the learning-teaching process, embedded in class activities and in the interactions between learners and between learners and teachers."

7. In recognizing the need to make proctored exams as convenient as possible to distance education students, Texas has established the Texas Computer-Based Testing Collaborative so that students can take them at a nearby educational institution or library. A similar program is in place with the sixty colleges and universities that participate in the Illinois Virtual Campus (Young, 2001).

8. A Gantt chart is a visual management tool that depicts progress on different parallel and sequential tasks of a project in relation to a horizontal time line. An American engineer named Henry Laurence Gantt (1861–1919) developed it.

9. In addition, every year a maintenance fee is assessed that is equal to 17 percent of the price of the server software and the total number of user licenses. Although eRoom Technology does not offer academic pricing, it does have volume discounting available.

10. The IDC study was sponsored by Mentergy, Inc. (www.mentergy.com), a new e-learning company formed by Gilat Communications after the acquisition of Allen Communication and the LearnLinc Corporation.

11. David F. Nobel (1998a, 1998b, 1998c), a history professor at York University, paints an appropriately grim picture in this regard. He has catalogued a number of instances where distance education programs have been initiated without the involvement or approval of faculty (see also Young, 1998, 2000a).

Chapter 2

1. It is important not to paint all forms of computer-based instruction with one brush. Without doubt, the most sophisticated and promising variant of computer-based instruction is the computer-based simulation. No one can dispute, for example, the learning value of a flight simulator in the training of pilots. Less expensive yet highly sophisticated simulation tools have been employed in corporate environments with success. The key to developing a sufficiently complex and challenging simulation is that it supports a strong probability of *failure* during the simulation process (Schank, 1997, pp. 29–39). No self-respecting video game can hold a player's attention if it can be mastered after one or two tries. Without

the experience of failure, users are denied the opportunity to learn from their mistakes in a "safe" environment. In a computer simulation, people do not lose their jobs by making a managerial blunder (or crashing the plane). Authentically complex simulations require considerable investment and may take years to complete. Beyond using mass-market simulation programs such as *SimCity 3000* in an urban economics or urban policy course, there is little opportunity to incorporate simulation programs effectively in the classroom. This will change eventually with advances in virtual reality technology and greater access to the *super*-broadband technologies of Internet2. Even so, the cost of producing such immersive simulations will likely approach that of the modern flight simulator—well beyond the budgetary reach of most institutions.

2. Of course, faculty also participate in asynchronous formats—primarily in discussion groups and e-mail correspondence. It is worth noting that the University of Illinois faculty seminar held in December 1999 concluded that distance education could bring about greater interaction between student and teacher than in the traditional classroom as long as the distance class was kept under about twenty-five.

3. For more on the debate over the ownership of on-line courses, see Carnevale and Young, 1999.

4. Stephen Ehrmann (1999) notes that one of the defining characteristics of the current educational revolution in e-learning is that both access and quality can be improved simultaneously. This parallels two previous revolutions in higher education: the use of reading and writing to extend the oral Socratic dialogue, and the development of the medieval university.

5. For example, the professor of a self-paced on-line course at the University of Iowa—which enrolled nineteen hundred students in the fall of 1999—was forced to issue failing midterm reports to more than half of them. Why? None had bothered even to start the course (Young, 1999a). For an interesting discussion on the problem of the dropout rate in distance education, see Carr (2000f). It seems likely that synchronous approaches to distance education, such as the broadband virtual classroom presented here, will be more successful in retaining students than the anytime, anywhere structure of most current formats.

6. The e-commerce dimension is already evident in the ongoing interest of commercial firms in campus Web site portals (see Looney and Lyman, 2000).

7. With the wholesale reevaluation of e-commerce that has taken place with the demise of many dot-com firms, assumptions about stickiness are also being questioned (see Weber, 2001).

8. The word *overt* is intended to suggest that there will be some e-commerce linkage. It seems clear that corporations will find it difficult to pass on opportunities to develop shopping portals in conjunction with employee initiatives involving the provision of computer hardware, software, peripherals, and Internet access. This e-commerce linkage may have nothing to do with educational offers per se but could be integrated into the corporate portal or "digital dashboard" established by the company. The concept of a digital dashboard has been the centerpiece of an array of knowledge-management initiatives by Microsoft (Gates, 1999; Gillmore and Angus, 1999b; Microsoft Corporation, 1999; Tebbe, 1999). The basic idea is to empower knowledge workers by providing access to everything they need to know on a single screen.

9. An interesting development to look for in the coming years will be on-line services that offer the equivalent of Priceline.com (that is, name your own price for an airplane ticket or hotel room and see if there are any takers) for residential college programs. A new service, called eCollegebid, is already trying to do this (Cooper, 2000; Gose 1999).

10. One Web site—Freescholarships.com—promised to give away a $10,000 scholarship every day (without any demonstration of academic promise or financial need) in order to attract high school and college students to the site (McCollum, 2000b). The site made its debut in February 2000 and went out of business seven months later (Haley, 2000).

11. Of course, no one dreams of trying to piece together a teaching career through an ad hoc collection of courses as an adjunct instructor either. Yet this is the prospect for many Ph.D. candidates today, particularly in the humanities. The economic prospects of many adjuncts could improve with the development of mass-produced education, given the likely strong demand for help desk personnel. Still, sitting in front of a computer monitor and fielding questions on someone else's lecture will be a dreary alternative to using one's own knowledge and creativity to put together a course.

Chapter 3

1. It should be noted that the licensing arrangements for QuickPlace would require either the purchase of additional QuickPlace licenses to accommodate these guest participants or the purchase of an extranet server license.

Chapter 4

1. I am indebted to Bates (2000, p. 12) for this example.

2. This approach will be less suitable for academic journals that are electronically available in full-text format through academic database subscriptions (for example, EBSCO Information Services). Publishers and journal aggregators will obviously want to sell journal subscriptions to each institution.

3. Many analysts believe that Moore's law will face an important obstacle by 2017—the finite size of the atom. But this is likely to turn out to be a minor bump in the road. For example, IBM recently announced that it has developed a quantum computer that uses the direction of an atom's spin for doing computations. IBM's quantum computer uses five flourine atoms in a specially designed molecule (Childi, 2000).

4. See Evans and Wurster (2000, pp. 64–65, 106–110) for the developing and important role of navigators in Internet-based economies.

5. It should be noted that the parent company of the University of Phoenix—the Apollo Group—has also entered into an agreement with Hughes to create a satellite-based distance education initiative ("University of Phoenix and Satellite-Technology Company," 1998).

6. One exceptionally quirky attempt to counter the way that video technology diminishes the instructor's classroom presence recently took place in a London high school classroom ("Professorial Apparition," 2000). In a distance education experiment, students entered their classroom to find a life-size holographic image of their mathematics teacher projected behind the lectern. Everyone in the room was transfixed by the remake of their mathematics teacher into the ghostly figure. The intent behind this so-called teleportational conferencing system was to stimulate eye contact and bring a more human touch to distance educa-

tion. Certainly, the battle for eye contact was won! But did the students learn anything and did this impart a more human touch? Probably not.

7. This pixel-splitting technology works best on an LCD screen because LCD pixels are perfect squares. Standard CRT monitors will also show some improvement, but it will not be as great, due to triangular positioning of the red, blue and green dots that make up each CRT pixel (Felici, 2000).

Chapter 5

1. Of course, extensive use of auctioning would likely have a demoralizing effect on both faculty and qualified students. That said, it should be noted that the admissions preferences accorded to children of alumni and notable benefactors could be viewed as a less overt expression of "purchasing" seats in the classroom.

2. One must also assume that the market for professional certification courses will be largely captured by mass-produced distance education. Such courses by their very nature are designed more to update particular knowledge domains than to explore new knowledge and skill sets.

3. I am grateful to Ted Marchese for this idea.

4. For institutions that adopt QuickPlace, this public Internet application would require the purchase of an extranet server license that allows an unlimited number of users to access the site.

REFERENCES

Agnew, Marion. "Collaboration on the Desktop: Web Conferencing and Instant Messaging Bring People Together." *InformationWeek*, July 10, 2000, pp. 87–88, 90, 92, 94.

Allee, Verna. *The Knowledge Evolution: Expanding Organizational Intelligence.* Boston: Butterworth-Heinemann, 1997.

Alwang, Greg. "Freedom of Speech." *PC Magazine*, February 8, 2000, p. 52.

Alwang, Greg. "Groove." *PC Magazine*, April 25, 2001. [www.zdnet.com/products/stories/reviews/0,4161,2706404,00.html]

Alwang, Greg. "Speech Recognition." *PC Magazine*, December 1, 1999, pp. 167–168, 174, 178, 180, 182, 188.

"Amazon.com Patent Covers Fee Program on Customer Referral." *Wall Street Journal*, February 28, 2000, p. A34.

Angwin, Julia. "Profit Eludes Priceline as Expansion Takes Its Toll." *Wall Street Journal*, January 25, 2001.

Ayres, Ian. "Lectures vs. Laptops." *New York Times*, March 20, 2001.

Bates, A. W. *Managing Technological Change: Strategies for College and University Leaders.* San Francisco: Jossey-Bass, 2000.

Beck, Rachel. "Amazon Unveils Purchase Circles, Showing Off Data Collection Tools." *Wall Street Journal*, August 20, 1999.

Berinato, Scott. "Ahead of the Pack." *University Business*, September 2000, pp. 32–38, 64–65.

Berkman, Robert. "Searching for the Right Search Engine." *Chronicle of Higher Education*, January 21, 2000, p. B6.

Bleed, Ron. "A Hybrid Campus for the New Millennium." *Educause Review*, 2001, *36*(1), 16–22, 24.

Block, Howard, and Dobell, Brandon. *The E-Bang Theory.* (monograph) Bank of America Securities, Education Industry Overview. September 1999.

Blumenstein, Rebecca. "How the Fiber Barons Plunged the U.S. Into a Telecom Glut." *Wall Street Journal,* June 18, 2001, pp. A1, A8.

Blumenstyk, Goldie. "Companies Find Academic Libraries a Key Target and a Tough Sell." *Chronicle of Higher Education,* May 18, 2001a, pp. A37–A38.

Blumenstyk, Goldie. "Harcourt's Virtual College Readies Launch." *Chronicle of Higher Education,* September 8, 2000a, p. A59.

Blumenstyk, Goldie. "Moving Beyond Textbook Sales, Harcourt Plans to Open a For-Profit University." *Chronicle of Higher Education,* June 4, 1999, p. A32.

Blumenstyk, Goldie. "On-Line Course Company Files for Bankruptcy." *Chronicle of Higher Education,* June 15, 2001b, p. A32.

Blumenstyk, Goldie. "Sale of Theses on Contentville Raises Hackles in U.S. and Canada." *Chronicle of Higher Education,* September 15, 2000b, pp. A37–A38.

Blumenstyk, Goldie. "Temple U. Shuts Down For-Profit Distance Education Company." *Chronicle of Higher Education,* July 23, 2001c, pp. A29–A30.

Blumenstyk, Goldie. "Thomson Will Close Harcourt's On-Line College." *Chronicle of Higher Education,* July 30, 2001d.

Blumenstyk, Goldie, and McCollum, Kelly. "Two Reports Question Utility and Accessibility in Distance Education." *Chronicle of Higher Education,* April 16, 1999, p. A31.

Bothun, Greg. "Cyberprof: The University in the Next Millennium." *Educom Review,* September-October 1999, *34*(5), 16–17.

Boyer, Ernest L. *Scholarship Reconsidered: Priorities of the Professoriate.* Princeton, N.J.: Carnegie Foundation for the Advancement of Teaching, 1990.

Bradley, Stephen, and Porter, Kelley. "eBay, Inc." Case 9–700–077. Boston, Mass.: Harvard Business School, 1999.

Bransford, John D., Brown, Ann L., and Cocking, Rodney R. (eds.). *How People Learn: Brain, Mind, Experience, and School.* Washington, D.C.: National Academy Press, 1999.

Bransten, Lisa. "NetLibrary Targets an Early Market for e-Books." *Wall Street Journal,* November 4, 1999, p. B12.

Bressler, Stacy E., and Grantham, Charles E., Sr. *Communities of Commerce: Building Internet Business Communities to Accelerate Growth, Minimize Risk, and Increase Customer Loyalty.* New York: McGraw-Hill, 2000.

Brooks, Peter. "Graduate Learning as Apprenticeship." *Chronicle of Higher Education,* December 20, 1996, p. A52.

Brooks, Rick. "Home Depot Plans to Move Gradually into Internet Sales." *Wall Street Journal,* August 30, 2000, p. B12.

Brown, Eric S. "Broadband Walks the Last Mile." [www.technologyreview.com/web/brown/brown060501.asp]. June 5, 2001.

Brown, John Seely. "Growing Up Digital: How the Web Changes Work, Education, and the Ways People Learn." *Change,* March-April 2000, *32*(2), 11–20.

Brown, John Seely, and Duguid, Paul. *The Social Life of Information.* Boston: Harvard Business School Press, 2000.

Brown, John Seely, and Duguid, Paul. "Universities in the Digital Age." *Change,* 1996, *28*(4), 11–19.

Brown, John Seely, Collins, Allan, and Duguid, Paul. "Situation Cognition and the Culture of Learning." *Educational Researcher,* 1989, *18*(1), 32–42.

Brown, Warren, and Swoboda, Frank. "Ford Offers Home PC to Every Employee." *Washington Post,* February 4, 2000, pp. A1, A12–A13.

Brownstein, Andrew. "Tuition Rises Faster Than Inflation, and Faster Than in Previous Year." *Chronicle of Higher Education,* October 27, 2000, p. A50.

Carlson, Scott. "12 Presses Join Online Venture." *Chronicle of Higher Education,* June 29, 2001, p. A31.

Carlson, Scott. "Universities Find Wireless Systems Bring Them Convenience and Savings." *Chronicle of Higher Education,* October 13, 2000a, p. A64

Carlson, Scott. "When Professors Create Software, Do They Own It, or Do Their Colleges?" *Chronicle of Higher Education,* July 21, 2000b, pp. A29, A31.

Carnevale, Dan. "Assessment Takes Center Stage in Online Learning." *Chronicle of Higher Education,* April 13, 2001a, pp. A43–A45.

Carnevale, Dan. "'Boot Camp' Helps New Online Students at Boise State University." *Chronicle of Higher Education,* February 18, 2000a, pp. A54–A55.

Carnevale, Dan. "Distance Education Can Bolster the Bottom Line, a Professor Argues." *Chronicle of Higher Education,* October 22, 1999a, p. A60.

Carnevale, Dan. "New Software Can Help to Grade Students' Online Essays." *Chronicle of Higher Education,* January 28, 2000b, p. A48.

Carnevale, Dan. "Senate Bill Would Help Online Instructors." *Chronicle of Higher Education,* June 22, 2001b, p. A32.

Carnevale, Dan. "University of Maryland University College Creates For-Profit Arm to Market Its On-Line Courses." *Chronicle of Higher Education,* December 17, 1999b, p. A49.

Carnevale, Dan. "Web Services Help Professors Detect Plagiarism." *Chronicle of Higher Education,* November 12, 1999c, p. A49.

Carnevale, Dan, and Young, Jeffrey R. "Who Owns On-Line Courses? Colleges and Professors Start to Sort It Out." *Chronicle of Higher Education,* December 17, 1999, pp. A45–A46.

Carr, Sarah. "A Company Helps Columbia and Harvard Put Some of Their Courses On-line." *Chronicle of Higher Education,* June 9, 2000d, p. A42.

Carr, Sarah. "A New Site Offers Free Courses, but First Students Must See Words from the Sponsors." *Chronicle of Higher Education,* June 16, 2000g, p. A39.

Carr, Sarah. "Another Web Company Eyes Academe, This One Offering Tutoring Assistance." *Chronicle of Higher Education,* December 3, 1999b, p. A45.

Carr, Sarah. "Army Plans to Offer Laptops and Distance Education to All Soldiers." *Chronicle of Higher Education,* July 14, 2000a, p. A44.

Carr, Sarah. "As Distance Education Comes of Age, the Challenge Is Keeping the Students: Colleges Are Using Online Courses to Raise Enrollment, but Retaining It Is Another Matter." *Chronicle of Higher Education,* February 11, 2000f, pp. A39–A41.

Carr, Sarah. "Closely Watched UNext Rolls Out Its First Courses." *Chronicle of Higher Education,* May 12, 2000b, p. A50.

Carr, Sarah. "Companies Use Online 'Universities' to Lure Customers." *Chronicle of Higher Education,* June 23, 2000c, p. A47.

Carr, Sarah. "Cornell Creates a For-Profit Subsidiary to Market Distance Education Programs." *Chronicle of Higher Education,* March 24, 2000e, p. A47.

Carr, Sarah. "Faculty Members Are Wary of Distance-Education Ventures." *Chronicle of Higher Education,* June 9, 2000h, p. A41–A42.

Carr, Sarah. "For-Profit Venture to Market Distance-Education Courses Stirs Concern at Temple." *Chronicle of Higher Education,* December 17, 1999a, pp. A46, A49.

Carr, Sarah. "Is Anyone Making Money on Distance Education?" *Chronicle of Higher Education,* February 16, 2001a, pp. A41–A43.

Carr, Sarah. "Lehigh Creates Online Courses for Admitted Applicants." *Chronicle of Higher Education*, February 18, 2000i, p. A56.

Carr, Sarah. "MIT Will Place Course Materials Online." *Chronicle of Higher Education*, April 20, 2001b, p. A54.

Carr, Sarah. "Princeton, Stanford, and Yale Plan Alliance to Offer Online Courses to Alumni." *Chronicle of Higher Education*, March 17, 2000j, p. A47.

Carr, Sarah. "Rich in Cash and Prestige, UNext Struggles in Its Search for Sales." *Chronicle of Higher Education*, May 4, 2001c, pp. A33–A35.

Carr, Sarah. "Two More Universities Start Diploma-Granting Virtual High Schools." *Chronicle of Higher Education*, December 10, 1999c, p. A49.

Carr, Sarah, and Kiernan, Vincent. "For-Profit Web Venture Seeks to Replicate the University Experience Online." *Chronicle of Higher Education*, April 14, 2000, pp. A59–A60.

Carr, Sarah, and Young, Jeffrey R. "As Distance-Learning Boom Spreads, Colleges Help Set Up Virtual High Schools." *Chronicle of Higher Education*, October 22, 1999, pp. A55–A58.

Carvajal, Doreen. "Racing to Convert Books to Bytes: Evolving Market for E-Titles." *New York Times*, December 9, 1999, p. C1.

Childi, George A. "Blowing Moore's Law to Bits." *InfoWorld*, August 15, 2000. [http://iwsun4.infoworld.com/articles/hn/xml/00/08/15/000815hnquantum.xml].

Chizmar, John F., and Williams, David B. "What Do Faculty Want?" *Educause Quarterly*, 2001, *24*(1), 18–24.

Clark, Don. "Microsoft to Ship Software That Makes Text on Computer Screens Look Clearer." *Wall Street Journal*, August 30, 1999, p. B6.

Coates, James. "Book Buying Enters New Chapter with Amazon.com." *Chicago Tribune*, October 10, 1999, p. 5 (Business Section).

Cohen, Adam. "The Attic of 'E'." *Time*, December 27, 1999, pp. 74–80.

Collins, Allan. "Cognitive Apprenticeship and Instructional Technology." In Lorna Idol and Beau Fly Jones (eds.), *Educational Values and Cognitive Instruction: Implications for Reform*. Hillsdale, N.J.: Erlbaum, 1991.

Collins, Allan, Brown, John Seely, and Newman, Susan E. "Cognitive Apprenticeship: Teaching the Crafts of Reading, Writing, and Mathematics." In Lauren B. Resnick (ed.), *Knowing, Learning, and Instruction: Essays in Honor of Robert Glaser*. Hillsdale, N.J.: Erlbaum, 1989.

Coopee, Todd. "Improved QuickPlace Suits Corporate Teams." *InfoWorld*, April 17, 2000, pp. 58, 60.

Cooper, Kenneth J. "For College, Name Your Price." *Washington Post*, February 7, 2000, p. A3.

Copeland, Ron. "Mine Your Intellectual Assets." *InformationWeek*, February 12, 2001, pp. 57, 60, 62, 64–65.

Costello, Sam. "Billion-Page Web Catalog Cited." *InfoWorld*, June 26, 2000. [http://iwsun4.infoworld.com/articles/hn/xml/00/06/26/000626hngoogle.xml].

Cox, Ana Marie. "Study Shows Colleges' Dependence on Their Part-Time Instructors." *Chronicle of Higher Education*, December 1, 2000, pp. A12, A14.

D'Amico, Mary Lisbeth. "Cisco CEO Sees E-Learning as Next Wave." *InfoWorld*, November 15, 1999. [http://www.infoworld.com/articles/pi/xml/99/11/16/991116pichambers.xml].

Daniel, John S. *Mega-Universities and Knowledge Media: Technology Strategies for Higher Education*. Guildford, U.K.: Biddles Ltd., 1996.

"A Distance-Learning Forecast Calls for Megaclasses." *Chronicle of Higher Education*, December 10, 1999, p. A47.

Ditlea, Steve. "The Real E–Books." *Technology Review*, July-August 2000, pp. 70–73, 76, 78.

Downes, Larry, and Mui, Chunka. *Unleashing the Killer App: Digital Strategies for Market Dominance*. Boston: Harvard Business School Press, 1998.

Drucker, David. "Collaboration Tool Aids MBA Courses." *InternetWeek*, November 29, 1999, p. 21–22.

Drucker, David. "Virtual Teams Light Up GE." *InternetWeek*, April 6, 2000, pp. 1, 16.

"Duke Business-School Venture Will Tailor Courses to Companies." *Chronicle of Higher Education*, July 14, 2000, p. A34.

Dvorak, John C. "The Myth of Broadband." *PC Magazine*, June 12, 2001, p. 85.

Ehrmann, Stephen C. "Access and/or Quality? Redefining Choices in the Third Revolution." *Educom Review*, September-October 1999, *34*(5), 24–27, 50–51.

Ellison, Sarah. "Internet Firms Shun Banner Ads in Favor of 'Affiliate Marketing.'" *Wall Street Journal*, July 10, 2000.

Entwistle, Noel. "Promoting Deep Learning Through Teaching and Assessment." In Linda Suskie (ed.), *Assessment to Promote Deep Learning*. Washington, D.C.: American Association for Higher Education, 2001.

Evans, Philip, and Wurster, Thomas S. *Blown to Bits: How the New Economics of Information Transforms Strategy*. Boston, Mass.: Harvard Business School Press, 2000.

Fallows, James. "From Your Lips to Your Printer." *Atlantic Monthly*, December 2000, pp. 106–108.

Farrington, Gregory C. "The New Technologies and the Future of Residential Undergraduate Education." In Richard N. Katz (ed.), *Dancing with the Devil: Information Technology and the New Competition in Higher Education*. San Francisco: Jossey-Bass, 1999.

Feenberg, Andrew. "No Frills in the Virtual Classroom" [www.aaup.org/SO99Feen.htm]. 1999.

Felici, James. "ClearType, CoolType: The Eyes Have It." Seybold Reports [www.adobe.com/epaper/features/cooltype/main.html]. 2000.

Forster, Stacy. "Online Brokers Try Bricks-and-Clicks." *Wall Street Journal*, February 12, 2001, p. A24.

Fosnot, Catherine Twomey (ed.). *Constructivism: Theory, Perspectives, and Practice*. New York: Teachers College Press, 1996.

Frayer, Dorothy A. "Creating a Campus Culture to Support a Teaching and Learning Revolution." *Cause/Effect*, 1999, *22*(2), 10–17, 50.

Freire, Paulo. *Pedagogy of the Oppressed*. New York: Continuum, 1995.

Fungaroli, Carole S. *Traditional Degrees for Nontraditional Students: How to Earn a Top Diploma from America's Great Colleges at Any Age*. New York: Farrar, Straus & Giroux, 2000.

Gajilan, Arlyn Tobias. "An Education Revolution." *Fortune*, March 2, 2001. [www.fsb.com/fortuneesb/articles/0,2227,1170,00.html].

Gants, David L. "Peer Review for Cyberspace: Evaluating Scholarly Web Sites." *Chronicle of Higher Education*, April 9, 1999, p. B8.

Gasaway, Laura N. "Distance Learning and Copyright: Is a Solution in Sight?" *Cause/Effect*, 1999, *22*(3), 6–8.

Gaskin, James E. "Groupware Gets Thin: A New Generation of Thin-Client Products Proves That Web Groupware Can Scale Across an Enterprise Network." *InternetWeek*, February 15, 2000, pp. 45, 47, 49.

Gates, Bill. *Business @ the Speed of Thought: Using a Digital Nervous System.* New York: Warner Books, 1999.

"Georgetown University Turns to Virtual Auctioneer to Offer Seats in a Course." *Chronicle of Higher Education,* January 21, 2000, p. A39.

Gilbert, Steven W. "A New Vision Worth Working Toward—Connected Education and Collaborative Change." [www.tltgroup.org/images/gilbert/NewVWWT2000/^NewVwwt2000—2–14–00.htm]. February 14, 2000.

Gillmore, Steve, and Angus, Jeff. "Digital Dashboard Offers Little Light." *Information Week,* October 25, 1999b, pp. 85–86, 90.

Gillmore, Steve, and Angus, Jeff. "Teamware Comes of Age." *Information Week,* September 20, 1999a, pp. 69, 72, 74, 78.

Givler, Peter. "Scholarly Books, the Coin of the Realm of Knowledge." *Chronicle of Higher Education,* November 12, 1999, p. A76.

Glasser, Perry. "A Medieval Strategy for a Digital Age." *Chronicle of Higher Education,* November 19, 1999, pp. B9–B10.

Gose, Ben. "Kaplan Starts Online Course on College-Admissions Process." *Chronicle of Higher Education,* January 14, 2000a, p. A53.

Gose, Ben. "Measuring the Value of an Ivy Degree." *Chronicle of Higher Education,* January 14, 2000b, pp. A52–A53.

Gose, Ben. "Web Site Lets Students Bid for a Degree." *Chronicle of Higher Education,* October 1, 1999, p. A55.

Gray, Matthew. "Measuring the Growth of the Web: June 1993 to June 1995." [www.mit.edu/people/mkgray/growth]. 1995.

Grenier, Melinda Patterson. "More People Have Access to Internet But Digital Divide Persists, Study Says." *Wall Street Journal,* February 18, 2001.

Griffiths, José-Marie. "Why the Web Is Not a Library." In Brian L. Hawkins and Patricia Battin (eds.), *The Mirage of Continuity: Reconfiguring Academic Information Resources for the 21st Century.* Washington, D.C.: Council on Library and Information Resources and Association of American Universities, 1998.

Grossberg, Michael. "Devising an Online Future for Journals of History." *Chronicle of Higher Education,* April 21, 2000, pp. B6–B7.

Guernsey, Lisa. "Distance Education for the Not-So-Distant: Colleges Debate the Wisdom of Having On-Campus Students Enroll in On-Line Classes." *Chronicle of Higher Education,* March 27, 1998a, pp. A29–A30.

Guernsey, Lisa. "Web Site Will Check Students' Papers Against Data Base to Detect Plagiarism." *Chronicle of Higher Education,* December 11, 1998b, p. A38.

Hagel, John, and Armstrong, Arthur G. *Net.Gain: Expanding Markets Through Virtual Communities.* Boston: Harvard Business School Press, 1997.

Haley, Colin C. "FreeScholarships.com Flunks: Site to Close, Workers Laid Off." [http://boston.internet.com/news/article/0,1928,2001_461831,00.html]. September 15, 2000.

Hamilton, David P. "No Substitute: The Internet Does NOT Change Everything." *Wall Street Journal,* March 12, 2001, p. R32.

Hamm, Steve. "The Wired Campus." *Business Week,* December 11, 2000, pp. EB104–EB106, EB108, EB110, EB113–EB115.

Hansell, Saul. "Free Rides Now Passé on Information Highway." *New York Times,* May 1, 2001a, pp. A1, C4.

Hansell, Saul. "Web Site Ads, Holding Sway, Start to Blare." *New York Times,* March 17, 2001b, pp. A1, C2.

Harasim, Linda M., Hiltz, Starr Roxanne, Teles, Lucio, and Turnoff, Murray. *Learning Networks.* Cambridge: MIT Press, 1995.

"Harvard to Offer Minicourses to Alumni." *Chronicle of Higher Education,* April 6, 2001, p. A41.

Hawkins, Brian L. "Technology, Higher Education, and a Very Foggy Crystal Ball." *Educause Review,* 2000, *35*(6), 64–66, 68, 70–73.

Hawkins, Brian L. "The Unsustainability of the Traditional Library and the Threat to Higher Education." In Brian L. Hawkins and Patricia Battin (eds.), *The Mirage of Continuity: Reconfiguring Academic Information Resources for the 21st Century.* Washington, D.C.: Council on Library and Information Resources and Association of American Universities, 1998.

Heck, Mike. "K-station Portal Brings New Life to Business Information." *InfoWorld,* February 5, 2001, p. 48.

Hine, Thomas. *The Rise and Fall of the American Teenager.* New York: Avon Books, 1999.

Hmelo, C. E. "Problem-Based Learning: Development of Knowledge and Reasoning Strategies." *Proceedings of the Seventeenth Annual Conference of the Cognitive Science Society* (pp. 404–408). Hillsdale, N.J.: Erlbaum, 1995.

Hogan, Kathleen, and Pressley, Michael. "Scaffolding Scientific Competencies within Classroom Communities of Inquiry." In Kathleen Hogan and Michael Pressley (eds.), *Scaffolding Student Learning: Instructional Approaches and Issues.* Cambridge, Mass.: Brookline Books, 1997.

IBM Redbooks. *Customizing QuickPlace.* Poughkeepsie, N.Y.: IBM Redbooks, 2000.

International Data Corporation. "eLearning in Practice: Blended Solutions in Action." [white paper]. Framingham, Mass.: International Data Corporation, 2000a.

International Data Corporation. "eLearning in Practice: Three Case Studies Sponsored by Mentergy Inc." [white paper]. Framingham, Mass.: International Data Corporation, 2000b.

"Internet's Birth Revamps Business and IT—Organizational Shift." *InfoWorld,* October 4, 1999, pp. 34, 36.

Jefferson, Steve. "Low–Cost, Flexible Displays Will Lighten Your Reading." *InfoWorld,* October 13, 2000, p. 104.

Jonassen, David H. *Computers in the Classroom: Mindtools for Critical Thinking.* Englewood Cliffs, N.J.: Prentice Hall, 1996.

Jonassen, David H., Peck, Kyle L, and Wilson, Brent G. *Learning with Technology: A Constructivist Perspective.* Englewood Cliffs, N.J.: Prentice Hall, 1998.

Jones, Jennifer. "Internet in the Sky Boosted." *InfoWorld,* July 11, 2000. [http://iwsun4.infoworld.com/articles/hn/xml/00/07/11/000711hnteledisic.xml].

Jones, Jennifer, and Briody, Dan. "AOL–Time Warner Deal to Boost Broadband Cable Net Access." *InfoWorld,* January 11, 2000. [www.infoworld.com/articles/en/xml/00/01/11/000111entimeaol.xml].

Jones, Jennifer, and Moore, Cathleen. "IT Finally Finds Its Voice: Telcos Pitch Voice/Data Convergence." *InfoWorld,* March 27, 2000, pp. 1, 32.

Kanter, Rosabeth Moss. *Evolve! Succeeding in the Digital Culture of Tomorrow.* Boston, Mass.: Harvard Business School Press, 2001.

Karabell, Zachary. *What's College For? The Struggle to Define American Higher Education*. New York: Basic Books, 1998.

Katz, Richard, and Associates. *Dancing with the Devil: Information Technology and the New Competition in Higher Education*. San Francisco: Jossey-Bass, 1999.

Katz, Stanley N. "In Information Technology, Don't Mistake a Tool for a Goal." *Chronicle of Higher Education*, June 15, 2001, pp. B7–B8.

Keating, Anne B., and Hargitai, Joseph. *The Wired Professor: A Guide to Incorporating the World Wide Web in College Instruction*. New York: New York University Press, 1999.

Kelly, Kevin. *New Rules for the New Economy: 10 Radical Strategies for a Connected World*. New York: Viking Penguin, 1998.

Kerr, Clark. *The Uses of the University* (4th ed.). Boston: Harvard University Press, 1995.

Kiely, Don. "XML Shows Great Promise for Server Development: Standard Provides Interchange Format for Distributed Apps." *InformationWeek*, May 3, 1999. [http://www.informationweek.com/732/32iuxml.htm].

Kiernan, Vincent. "An Ambitious Plan to Sell Electronic Books: University Librarians and Press Officials See Promise and Possible Pitfalls in the Concept." *Chronicle of Higher Education*, April 16, 1999a, p. A29.

Kiernan, Vincent. "Rewards Remain Dim for Professors Who Pursue Digital Scholarship: A Case Study at Indiana University Shows That Ways to Evaluate Online Work Are Still Lacking." *Chronicle of Higher Education*, April 28, 2000, pp. A45–A46.

Kiernan, Vincent. "Why Do Some Electronic-Only Journals Struggle, While Others Flourish? Visibility Looms Large for Authors Seeking a Publisher for Their Papers." *Chronicle of Higher Education*, May 21, 1999b, pp. A25–A27.

Kronholz, June. "Why Has Senior Year of High School Lost Its Purpose for Many?" *Wall Street Journal*, March 23, 1999, pp. A1, A13.

Kyrillidou, Martha. "Trends in ARL Libraries: Introduction to ARL Statistics, 1998–99." Washington, D.C.: Association of Research Libraries, 2000.

Lange, Katherine. "History in a New Medium: Web Replaces Term Papers in Class." *Wall Street Journal* (Interactive Edition), December 14, 2000.

Lave, Jean, and Wenger, Etienne. *Situated Learning: Legitimate Peripheral Participation*. New York: Cambridge University Press, 1993.

Leatherman, Courtney. "Part-Timers Continue to Replace Full-Timers on College Faculties." *Chronicle of Higher Education*, January 28, 2000, pp. A18–A19.

Leibowitz, Wendy. "Alumni Offices Use Electronic Media to Forge Closer Ties with Graduates." *Chronicle of Higher Education*, October 15, 1999, pp. A45–A46.

Lenzner, Robert, and Johnson, Stephen S. "Seeing Things As They Really Are." *Forbes*, March 10, 1997, pp. 122–128.

Levin, Carol. "A New Chapter for E-Books." *PC Magazine*, January 4, 2000, p. 36.

Lipnack, Jessica, and Stamps, Jeffrey. *Virtual Teams: Reach Across Space, Time, and Organizations with Technology*. New York: Wiley, 1997.

Lockee, Barbara, Moore, Mike, and Burton, John. "Old Concerns with New Distance Education Research." *Educause Quarterly*, 2001, *24*(2), 60–62.

Looney, Michael, and Lyman, Peter. "Portals in Higher Education." *Educause Review*, July-August 2000, pp. 28–34, 36.

Loose, Cindy. "Online Education to Be Free." *Washington Post*, March 15, 2000, pp. A1, A13.

Magner, Denise K. "The Imminent Surge in Retirements." *Chronicle of Higher Education*, March 17, 2000, pp. A18–A20.

Mandel, Michael J., and Hof, Robert D. "Rethinking the Internet." *BusinessWeek*, March 26, 2001, pp. 116–122.

Mannion, Patrick. "Intel Sees E–Learning as Next Killer App." [http://content.techweb.com/wire/story/TWB20010406S0005]. April 6, 2001.

Marchese, Theodore J. "New Conversations About Learning: Insights from Neuroscience and Anthropology, Cognitive Science and Work-Place Studies." In AAHE, *Assessing Impact: Evidence and Action*. Washington, D.C.: American Association for Higher Education, 1997.

Markoff, John. "Microsoft is Ready to Supply a Phone in Every Computer." *New York Times*, June 12, 2001, pp. A1, C15.

Marlowe, Bruce A., and Page, Marilyn L. *Creating and Sustaining the Constructivist Classroom.* Thousand Oaks, Calif.: Corwin Press, 1998.

Marsan, Carolyn Duffy. "XML Search Engine to Ship." *InfoWorld*, April 14, 2000. [http://www.infoworld.com/articles/ic/xml/00/04/14/000414icxml.xml].

McCollum, Kelly. "Company Plans Web-Based Study Guides for Survey-Level Courses." *Chronicle of Higher Education,* January 14, 2000a, p. A49.

McCollum, Kelly. "Site Seeks to Draw Students by Offering a $10,000 Scholarship Every Day." *Chronicle of Higher Education*, February 3, 2000b.

McCormick, John. "The New School: An Ambitious Start-Up with Blue-Chip University Partners and Very Deep Pockets Hopes to Bring College to Millions Worldwide—and Transform the Way They Learn." *Newsweek*, April 24, 2000, pp. 60–62.

McDougall, Paul. "Groove Networks' Software to Aid in Collaboration." *InformationWeek*, October 30, 2000, p. 26.

McGee, Marianne Kolbasuk. "Colleges Master Online Learning." *InformationWeek*. [www.informationweek.com/826/elearning_side.htm]. February 26, 2001.

Mehta, Stephanie N., and Chen, Kathy. "U.S. Market for Broadband Is Barely Tapped." *Wall Street Journal,* January 12, 2000, p. B8.

Merisotis, Jamie P., and Phipps, Ronald A. "What's the Difference? Outcomes of Distance vs. Traditional Classroom-Based Learning." *Change*, May-June 1999, *31*(3), 12–17.

Metcalfe, Bob. "Microsoft, Internet Stocks, Residential Broadband, Y2K, and AOL-Time Warner." *InfoWorld*, January 24, 2000, p. 102.

Microsoft Corporation. "Practicing Knowledge Management: Turning Experience and Information into Results." Microsoft Knowledge Management Strategy White Paper, 1999. [www.microsoft.com/Business/km/resources/kmpract.asp].

Moozakis, Chuck. "Ulterior E-Motives: Employee PC Giveaways Aim to Deliver Revenue." *InternetWeek*, February 14, 2000, pp. 1, 64.

National Commission on the High School Senior Year. "The Lost Opportunity of Senior Year: Finding a Better Way." [www.commissiononthesenioryear.org/Report/report.html]. January 2001.

National Public Radio. "Talk of the Nation," October 18, 1999.

Neal, Ed. "Using Technology in Teaching: We Need to Exercise Healthy Skepticism." *Chronicle of Higher Education,* June 19, 1998, pp. B4–B5.

"New Book Says College Is for Everyone—as Long as It Isn't Virtual. *Chronicle of Higher Education*, November 12, 1999, p. A47.

Noble, David F. "Digital Diploma Mills, Part II: The Coming Battle over Online Instruction." [http://communication.ucsd.cdu/dl/ddm2.html]. March 1998b.

Noble, David F. "Digital Diploma Mills, Part III: The Bloom Is off the Rose."
[www.vpaa.uillinois.edu/tid/resources/noble.html]. November 1998c.

Noble, David F. "Digital Diploma Mills: The Automation of Higher Education." *First Monday*, January 1998a, *3*(1). [www.firstmonday.dk/issues/3_1/noble/index.html].

O'Donnell, James J. *Avatars of the Word: From Papyrus to Cyberspace*. Cambridge, Mass.: Harvard University Press, 1998.

O'Leary, Mick. "NetLibrary: The Virtual Library Arrives?" *Information Today*, September 1999, *16*(8), 15–16.

O'Neill, James M. "Making MIT Course Material Available on Net is Savvy Marketing." *Philadelphia Inquirer*, April 8, 2001, p. E3.

Olsen, Florence. "Colleges Weigh Legal Action Against Web Sites That Publish Lecture Notes." *Chronicle of Higher Education*, November 26, 1999, p. A69.

Olsen, Florence. "The Wireless Revolution." *Chronicle of Higher Education*, October 13, 2000b, pp. A59–A61.

Olsen, Florence. "Two California Digital Libraries Agree to Collaborate on Online Projects." *Chronicle of Higher Education*, June 14, 2000a.

Palloff, Rena M., and Pratt, Keith. *Building Learning Communities in Cyberspace: Effective Strategies for the Online Classroom*. San Francisco: Jossey-Bass, 1999.

Paskey, Janice. "Online Peacekeeping Program Includes a Trip to Bosnia." *Chronicle of Higher Education*, August 18, 2000, p. A40.

Pasztor, Andy. "Hughes Aims to Expand AOL Satellite Venture." *Wall Street Journal*, January 14, 2000, p. B2.

Pasztor, Andy. "Hughes, Lockheed Fail to Find Sponsors for Satellite Projects." *Wall Street Journal* (Interactive Version), June 4, 2001.

Payne, Doug. "A Revolutionary Idea in Publishing." *Chronicle of Higher Education*, March 9, 2001, pp. A39–A40.

Pelikan, Jaroslav. *The Idea of the University: A Reexamination*. New Haven, Conn.: Yale University Press, 1992.

Perillo, Lucia. "When the Classroom Becomes a Confessional." *Chronicle of Higher Education*, November 28, 1997, p. A56.

"Pew Survey Disputes Notion That Net Encourages Isolation." *Wall Street Journal*, May 10, 2000.

Piaget, Jean. *Equilibration of Cognitive Structures*. New York: Viking, 1977.

Piaget, Jean. *Structuralism*. New York: Basic Books, 1970.

Pillemer, David B., Picariello, Martha L., Law, Anneliesa Beebe, and Reichman, Jill S. "Memories of College: The Importance of Specific Educational Episodes." In David C. Rubin (ed.), *Remembering Our Past: Studies in Autobiographical Memory*. New York: Cambridge University Press, 1996.

Polivka, Bryan, and Patterson, John. "Caliber Design and Delivery: The Complete Service Solution." Baltimore, Md.: Caliber Learning Network, 1999.

Porter, Lynnette R. *Creating the Virtual Classroom: Distance Learning with the Internet*. New York: Wiley, 1997.

Prencipe, Loretta W. "Do You Know the Rules and Manners of an Effective Virtual Meeting?" *InfoWorld*, April 30, 2001, p. 46.

Press, Eyal, and Washburn, Jennifer. "The Kept University." *Atlantic Monthly*, March 2000, pp. 39–42, 45–52, 54.

Pringle, David. "Europe Web Providers Rev Up Shopping Engines." *Wall Street Journal,* December 13, 1999, p. B33.

"Professorial Apparition Enhances Remote Teaching." *Chronicle of Higher Education,* February 25, 2000, p. A49.

Quittner, Joshua. "An Eye on the Future." *Time,* December 27, 1999, pp. 56–64, 66.

Raish, Martin. "Academic Librarians Offer the Crucial Human Element in Online Scholarship." *Chronicle of Higher Education,* April 21, 2000, pp. B4–B5.

Reid, T. R. "New College Topic in Britain: Tuition." *Washington Post,* January 10, 1999, p. A20.

Rewick, Jennifer L. "Britannica Moves to Capture More of Online Market." *Wall Street Journal,* October 19, 1999, p. B5.

Richtel, Matt. "E-Commerce Dream Proves the Undoing of a Solid Business." *New York Times,* November 24, 2000, pp. A1, A44.

Rogoff, Barbara. *Apprenticeship in Thinking: Cognitive Development in Social Context.* New York: Oxford University Press, 1990.

Romero, Simon. "Once-Bright Future of Optimal Fiber Dims." *New York Times,* June 18, 2001, p. A1.

Rose, Matthew. "Brill's Contentville Runs into Internet Copyright Wall." *Wall Street Journal,* August 3, 2000, p. B4.

Rowley, Daniel James, Lujan, Herman D., and Dolence, Michael G. *Strategic Choices for the Academy: How Demand for Lifelong Learning Will Re-Create Higher Education.* San Francisco: Jossey-Bass, 1998.

Russakoff, Dale. "Mind Games for Tech Success: You've Got to Play to Win." *Washington Post,* May 8, 2000, pp. A1, A4.

Sapp, Geneva. "Audio Talk, eFusion Ring VOIP." *InfoWorld,* January 31, 2000, p. 16.

Scannell, Ed, and Harreld, Heather. "Groove Breathes Real Life into P-to-P." *InfoWorld,* April 16, 2001, p. 12.

Schank, Roger. "A Vision of Education for the 21st Century." *T.H.E. Journal,* January 2000, pp. 43–45.

Schank, Roger. *Virtual Learning: A Revolutionary Approach to Building a Highly Skilled Workforce.* New York: McGraw-Hill, 1997.

Schiesel, Seth. "AOL Plans the Digital Smorgasbord." *New York Times,* June 11, 2001, p. A1.

Schneider, Alison. "To Many Adjunct Professors, Academic Freedom Is a Myth." *Chronicle of Higher Education,* December 10, 1999, pp. A18–A19.

Schumpeter, Joseph. *Capitalism, Socialism, and Democracy.* New York: HarperCollins, 1942.

Schwartz, John, and Dobrzynski, Judith. "Three Men are Charged with Fraud in 1,100 Art Actions on EBay." *New York Times,* March 9, 2001, p. A1.

Shachtman, Noah. "Precision Searches: Custom-Tailored Search Tools Are Helping E-Commerce Sites Improve Their Customer Service, Trim Costs and, Hopefully, Boost Revenue." *InternetWeek,* December 6, 1999, pp. 53, 60, 62.

Shapiro, Carl, and Varian, Hal R. *Information Rules: A Strategic Guide to the Network Economy.* Boston: Harvard Business School Press, 1999.

Shenk, David. *Data Smog: Surviving the Information Glut.* San Francisco: HarperEdge, 1997.

Skinner, B. F. *Science and Human Behavior.* New York: Free Press, 1953.

"Software Magnate's Distance-Learning Venture Will Proceed, He Says." *Chronicle of Higher Education,* February 23, 2001, p. A34.

Spiwak, Rand. "The Technology Refresh Program: Affording State-of-the-Art Personal Computing." *Educause Quarterly*, 2000, *23*(1), 56–58.

Steinberg, Jacques. "As Teacher in the Classroom, Internet Needs Fine-Tuning." *New York Times*, July 7, 2000a, pp. A1, A12

Steinberg, Jacques. "For Gatekeepers at Colleges, a Daunting Task of Weeding." *New York Times*, February 27, 2000b, pp. A1, A30.

Streitfeld, David. "Advertising on Internet Doesn't Click." *Washington Post*, October 29, 2000, p. A1.

Streitfeld, David, and Cha, Ariana Eunjung. "Dot-Coms Pull Back on Internet Freebies." *Washington Post*, March 18, 2001, p. A1.

Struckman, Robert. "Boulder-Based Site Has Classics." *Denver Post*, May 16, 2000, p. E1.

"Students Weave Web Authoring Dreams at Wake Forest." *T.H.E. Journal*, June 1999, p. 8.

Swanson, Sandra. "E–Learning Branches Out." *InformationWeek*, February 26, 2001, pp. 42–44, 48, 50, 54, 56, 58, 60.

Sweat, Jeff. "Ask Jeeves to Let Customers Talk to Service Reps." *InformationWeek*, March 6, 2000.

Swisher, Kara. "Content on Web is Under Fire for Losing Cash." *Wall Street Journal*, October 9, 2000, p. B1.

Talbott, Stephen. "Who's Killing Higher Education." *Educom Review*, March-April 1999, *34*(2), 26–30, 32–33.

Tebbe, Mark. "No, Those Aren't Documents, They're 'Knowledge Sources': Lotus, Microsoft to Battle for the Next Business Tool." *InfoWorld*, April 19, 1999, p. 30.

Teles, Lucio. "Cognitive Apprenticeship on Global Networks." In Linda M. Harasim (ed.), *Global Networks: Computers and International Communication*. Cambridge, Mass.: MIT Press, 1993.

Thurston, Scott. "Delta Offers Home Computers to 72,000 Workers." *Atlanta Journal-Constitution*, February 4, 2000, p. 10A.

Tillett, L. Scott. "E–Businesses Are Bringing Voice to the Web." *InternetWeek*, November 6, 2000.

Toby, Jackson. "Cakewalk to College." *Washington Post*, March 2, 2000, p. A19.

Traub, James. "This Campus Is Being Simulated." *New York Times Magazine*, November 19, 2000, pp. 88–93, 113–114, 118, 125–126.

Twigg, Carol A. "Improving Learning and Reducing Costs: Redesigning Large-Environment Courses." Pew Symposia in Learning and Technology. [www.center.rpi.edu/PewSym/mono1.html]. 1999.

Ubell, Robert. "Who Owns What? Unbundling Web Course Property Rights." *Educause Quarterly*, 2001, *24*(1), 45–47.

University of Illinois Faculty Seminar, "Teaching at an Internet Distance: The Pedagogy of Online Teaching and Learning." December 7, 1999.

"University of Phoenix and Satellite-Technology Company to Team Up." *Chronicle of Higher Education*, September 4, 1998, p. A37.

"University of Phoenix Reports Enrollment Growth on Land and Online." *Chronicle of Higher Education*, July 7, 2000, p. A29.

U.S. Department of Education. *Highlights from the Third International Mathematics and Science Study.* (NCES 1999–081). Washington, D.C.: U.S. Department of Education, Office of Educational Research and Improvement, 1999.

Vygotsky, Lev S. *Mind in Society.* Cambridge, U.K.: Cambridge University Press, 1978.

Vygotsky, Lev S. *Thought and Language.* Cambridge, Mass.: MIT Press, 1986.

Wagner, Mitch. "Free-PC Programs: Where's the Payback?" *InternetWeek*, April 23, 2001, pp. 1, 48.

Walker, Deborah, and Lambert, Linda. "Learning and Leading Theory: A Century in the Making." In Linda Lambert, Deborah Walker, Diane P. Zimmerman, Joanne E. Cooper, Morgan Dale Lambert, Mary E. Gardner, and P. J. Ford Slack (eds.), *The Constructivist Leader*. New York: Teachers College Press, 1995.

Weber, Tom. "A 'Sticky' Situation: How a Web Buzzword Spun Out of Control." *Wall Street Journal*, March 5, 2001, p. B1.

Weber, Tom. "In the Age of Napster, Protecting Copyright Is a Digital Arms Race." *Wall Street Journal*, July 24, 2000a, p. B1.

Weber, Tom. "Protecting Copyrights: How E-Books Will Be Like Parking Meters." *Wall Street Journal*, September 11, 2000b, p. B1.

Weigel, Van B. "E-Learning and the Tradeoff Between Richness and Reach in Higher Education." *Change*, 2000a, *32*(5), 10–15.

Weigel, Van B. "Free Degrees? They're Only a Matter of Time." *Chronicle of Higher Education*, May 19, 2000b, p. B8.

Wenger, Etienne. *Communities of Practice: Learning, Meaning, and Identity*. Cambridge: Cambridge University Press, 1998.

Wenger, Etienne C., and Snyder, William M. "Communities of Practice: The Organizational Frontier." *Harvard Business Review*, January-February 2000, pp. 139–145.

"Wharton Earns an ASP Degree." *InformationWeek*, October 25, 1999, p. 17.

"Wharton's Undergrads Get Business Experience in 'Virtual Meeting Room.'" *Business Wire*, November 1, 1999.

White, Erin. "Washington Post Stays the Course with Web Operations." *Wall Street Journal*, February 2, 2000, p. B4.

Wilde, Candee. "Telework Programs Speed Up: High-Speed Access Technologies Like Cable Modems and DSL Give Telecommuting a Lift." *InternetWeek*, April 17, 2000, pp. 40, 42.

Wilgoren, Jodi. "Invasion of Laptops Spurs a Revolution in College Teaching." *New York Times*, March 26, 2000, p. A1.

Willdorf, Nina. "Music Educators Put Recordings Online, Warily." *Chronicle of Higher Education*, May 26, 2000, p. A53.

Willmott, Don. "The Top 100 Web Sites and the Technologies That Make Them Work." *PC Magazine*, February 8, 2000, pp. 144–158.

Wingfield, Nick. "Amazon.com to Sell E-Books in Format from Microsoft." *Wall Street Journal*, August 29, 2000, p. B12.

Wingfield, Nick. "Ebay Allows Sellers to Set Up 'Storefronts' On-line in Bid to Expand Beyond Auctions." *Wall Street Journal*, June 12, 2001.

Winston, Gordon C., and Zimmerman, David J. "Where Is Aggressive Price Competition Taking Higher Education?" *Change*, July-August 2000, *32*(4), 10–18.

Wood, David, Bruner, Jerome S., and Ross, Gail. "The Role of Tutoring in Problem Solving." *Journal of Child Psychology and Psychiatry and Allied Disciplines*, 1976, *17*, 89–100.

Young, Jeffrey R. "David Noble's Battle to Defend the 'Sacred Space' of the Classroom." *Chronicle of Higher Education*, March 31, 2000a, pp. A47–A49.

Young, Jeffrey R. "Distance and Classroom Education Seen as Equally Effective." *Chronicle of Higher Education*, February 18, 2000b, p. A55.

Young, Jeffrey R. "Distance Education Transforms Help Desks Into '24-7' Operations." *Chronicle of Higher Education*, May 26, 2000c, pp. A49–A50.

Young, Jeffrey R. "Moving the Seminar Table to the Computer Screen: Liberal-Arts Colleges Experiment with Online Collaboration." *Chronicle of Higher Education,* July 7, 2000d, pp. A33–A34.

Young, Jeffrey R. "Skeptical Academics See Perils in Information Technology." *Chronicle of Higher Education,* May 8, 1998, pp. A29–A30.

Young, Jeffrey R. "Students' F's Highlight Problems in Electronic Course at U. of Iowa." *Chronicle of Higher Education,* November 26, 1999a, p. A67.

Young, Jeffrey R. "Texas Colleges Collaborate to Offer Online Students Convenient Proctored Tests." *Chronicle of Higher Education,* March 9, 2001, p. A43.

Young, Jeffrey R. "Three Top Research Libraries Plan Vast, New Facility to Store Little-Used Books." *Chronicle of Higher Education,* April 30, 1999b, p. A26.

INDEX